A No-nonsense Guide to Organizing Your Home:

Declutter, Destress, Save Time, Money, and Fall in Love With Your Home Again

Kira Kendal
GP Global Publishing

Copyright © 2023 by Kira Kendal/GP Publishing

All rights reserved.

No part of this publication may be reproduced, distributed, or transmitted in any form or by any means without the prior written permission of the publisher, except for brief quotations embodied in critical reviews and other noncommercial uses permitted by U.S copyright law.

All content, text, images, graphics, logos, and materials in this publication are the property of GP Publishing unless otherwise stated. Unauthorized use or reproduction of copyrighted materials is strictly prohibited and may violate copyright laws. For permissions or inquiries, please contact Kira Kendal at gp.publishing@gmail.com.

The information provided in this publication is for general informational purposes only. We make no warranties about the reliability, or completeness of the information. We are not liable for any loss or damage resulting from the use of this publication.

We reserve the right to modify this copyright page without prior notice.

Thank you for respecting our copyright and intellectual property rights.

"FOR EVERY MINUTE SPENT IN ORGANIZING, AN HOUR IS EARNED"

Benjamin Franklin

Contents

1. Introduction 1
2. Statistics to Inspire Action 10
3. Assessing the Present Condition 18
4. Create a Plan to fit your life 23
5. Declutter Then Organize Room by Room 33
6. Tackling Junk Drawers 37
7. Home Office 40
8. Hallways 45
9. Living Room/Family Room 48
10. Kitchen 53

11.	Laundry Room	62
12.	Bedroom Closets	65
13.	Bedrooms	71
14.	Bathrooms	83
15.	Children's Bedrooms and Playrooms	87
16.	Linen, Coat, and Hall Closets	92
17.	Papers and Digital Information	100
18.	Attic, Basement, Garage	115
19.	Outdoor Spaces- Lawn, Porches, Patios and Sheds	128
20.	Options for junk removal	141
21.	Plan for Maintaining Order	151
22.	Conclusion	158
23.	Bonus Chapter: Cleaning Solutions	165
Additional Statistics		185
Free Planner Access Link and QR Code		191
Acknowledgements		193
About Author		198

Introduction

Welcome to the world of

home organization!

We have a life with real-life issues and responsibilities to deal with. Please remember that being done is better than being perfect. Each step will lead you to an improved sanctuary for you and your family to delight in. A cluttered space causes anxiety and stress. An organized home can bring a sense of calm and tranquility.

Whether you live in a tiny apartment or a large two-story house, managing your home is vital for creating a functional and enjoyable living space you will love as much as when you first moved in. I speak from my experience living with clutter and too much stuff for too long.

6 Ways clutter affects you and your family

1. **Causes undue stress** - stepping over clutter and going through piles of paper cause more stress than you think.

2. **Ransacks homes** - inability to find storage due to the high volume of items you own

3. **wastes time** - looking for lost items

4. **This leads to overspending** - impulse buying and emotional purchases are common for those that live with clutter.

5. **Depletes energy** - energy zappers are unfinished to-do lists and the constant visual reminder of things to be done.

6. **Robs you of peace** – it can be challenging to rest and relax in chaos; the human brain likes order.

According to WebMD, too much stuff can damage your physical and mental health.

Older Adults with too much stuff are more apt to delay making decisions about what to get rid of than younger people. It is more challenging for your brain to focus if your environment is disorganized. It is even harder for those who have ADHD.

Knickknacks, also known as "dust collectors," make it harder to keep your spaces clean. This can directly increase sneezing, itchy eyes, and wheezing for anyone with allergies. A tidy house feels inviting for those who live there and their guests. Shutting out people because of this can make you feel sad and lonely and take a toll on relationships.

The risks of getting injured are more significant when you live with lots of clutter. Boxes, piles of clothing, or even too much furniture makes it that much easier to trip and fall.

This guide includes helpful tips and tricks for decluttering, organizing, and maintaining your home. I want to help you manage your things, not ask you to become a minimalist and eliminate everything you love and desire. There are other books with that goal in mind.

I want to help you get the most out of all your rooms and spaces with simple and inexpensive solutions. I'm hoping you find a process that works for you. You'll learn to maximize your area, create storage solutions, and streamline your daily routines. Implementing the organizing principles simplify your life, saving time and money.

Challenges you will face on this journey:

- Procrastination in taking that first step.

- Reluctance to let go of items collected over time that are forgotten or unnecessary in your day-to-day life.

- Getting family members' cooperation.

Just because you have a place for an object is not a reason to keep it. Always ask, do you need it or enjoy it in your current life? Keep in mind that taking the first step is the hardest part.

I moved forward by starting small and building on that. Do this process at your own pace and revel in each accomplishment as you go.

If we are honest, we are not all fortunate enough to afford a professional organizer for our home. I'm very happy for those who can, but I'm one of the many who cannot. Are you a busy Mom, a working mother, or possibly a single parent?

You're not alone if you are overwhelmed with clutter or drowning in laundry. What about that sink that always seems full of dirty dishes or a dining table cluttered with mail or folded laundry that never seems to get put away?

A considerable percentage of people are unhappy about how their home is organized. That was me before I started this book. Suppose you are one of those who never seem to have extra time. In that case, the statistics in the following chapter may convince you to work on organizing your home and what it can mean to you and your family. Once you get more organized, you will feel less stressed and have more time and money.

Decluttering before cleaning an area will always make the job much easier. Step one in this journey is to remove all accumulated trash in the area. You don't have to declutter and get rid of everything you love.

When you start the job, be honest with yourself about what makes you happy or what you need or want in each area. Then, let go of the rest. Don't keep that awful vase you hate because Aunt Maggie gave it to you. If it makes you remember Aunt Maggie, take a picture to keep with Aunt Maggie's photos. Taking photos of some of the items may help with letting go of things yet can preserve the memory, and digital images will keep your spaces neat. This might make it much easier to let go. If you don't love it in your room, let go of the clutter, but preserved the memory. Another option is moving it to an area better suited if you want to keep it.

The decluttering step was challenging for me as part of the entire process, so that is where this book will start. This is not just a one-time and then-done but an ongoing process to create a home where you can find more efficiency, peace of mind, and relaxation.

If you are a sentimental person, some things have special meaning to you. You may not be a candidate for minimalism, and that's OK. I certainly am not. Make your organized home fit your life. Remember that every life is unique, and you and your family are too.

Those things you have and love should have a home where they are displayed, which will bring you happiness each time you see them. Determine if you have a collection or if it is just clutter. Also, make your life easier by storing the items you use frequently in places near where they are used. Let's dive in and create a beautiful, organized home you and your family will love!

The next chapter is about statistics on the benefits of decluttering and organizing. Some love statistics, and some find them an awful bore. If you are not interested in those, skip the chapter and get started on your first task. I found the information interesting, motivating, and eye-opening. If interested, consider the facts and see how your home zaps you of the energy and time to do what you want. Now put together your personal plan of action and begin.

STATISTICS TO INSPIRE ACTION

Let's look at some of those statistics and apply them to how we feel about our homes. The average size of a home in America has continually increased over the years. The average number of items in these homes is 300,000. An average of 20% of the items we own are things we frequently use.

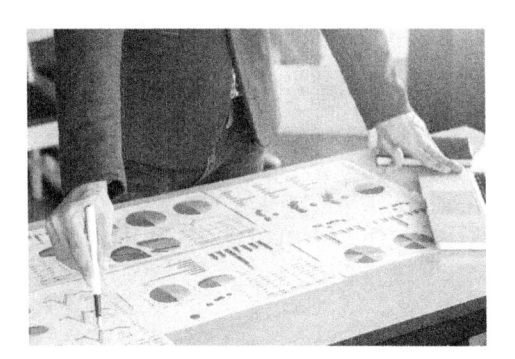

According to several surveys, the most often misplaced items are keys, tv remotes, phones, glasses, and shoes. Think about how much time and stress could be eliminated when getting ready to go out by keeping these items in a designated place. The amount of time searching for a lost item is usually 1 to 10 minutes. I have spent up to 30 minutes looking for my keys or purse. This is a real problem when you have an appointment.

These sound like small amounts of time but add up to large chunks of time wasted. What could you do with an extra hour daily if you were more organized? A report from The National Association of Professional Organizers (NAPO) states that most of us look for lost and misplaced items for a year of our lives.

That amounts to 8,700 hours of our lives. How would you like to get a year of wasted time back? That's time you could spend doing what you love instead.

How do you feel when you open your closet? Around 10% of American women admit they are unhappy when they open that door and feel depressed. Most admitted that the reason was that the closet never seemed organized the way they wanted and also that they didn't like trying to figure out where their favorite things were located.

Thousands of women admit they have the same issue, so learning how to organize your closet is handy. According to many women, something as simple as a shoe organizer is one of the most useful things in your closet. Three out of ten women have said that having an organized closet results in a much less stressful morning. A good start leads to a more productive and less stressful day. A study of 2,137 U.S. women revealed that their closets had an average of $550 worth of unworn clothing (10Yetis survey).

How often have you been late to work because of clutter and disorganization? More than 50% feel that their life is overwhelmed with clutter in their homes and don't know how to deal with it or fix the problem.

There is an entire organization industry available to assist with all these issues. That market size had increased to an 11.4 billion dollar business by 2020 and is continually growing by approximately 4% yearly. An average home organizer charges $55/hour for their services. The jobs can range from $540 to $1,000 for more complicated jobs. Unfortunately, most Americans do not have a budget for this type of service. This book is written for those of you who desire to do the job on your own, at your own pace and lays out steps and suggestions to help you be successful.

Decluttering trends and statistics that you should be aware of and can help you include the fact that up to 12% of us admit that we worry about how cluttered our homes are when we have guests.

Before the pandemic, lots of us used spare rooms for storage. When Covid required us to work from home, some of those spaces were converted to home offices, and we lost that storage space. Rather than sort through the things in the room, most just shifted all that to another area creating a more cluttered environment.

There have been many studies that show a direct connection between your happiness and having a decluttered space. Most of us are also more productive and less stressed in a less cluttered space. We feel more like socializing with friends and family at home when we are not stressed about the clutter surrounding us. According to the Centers for Disease Control, 80% of medical spending is related to stress compared to other issues.

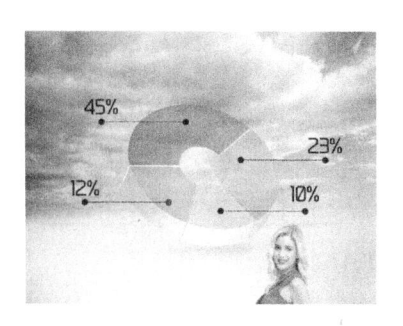

Almost a quarter of adults (23%) admit to paying bills late because they are lost or misplaced. That number is according to Consumer Agencies and a Harris Interactive report. Is that you?

You can increase your budget instantly by paying the minimum or more on time.

Who can't use more money, right? Late charges add up fast if you have multiple cards. Utilities also add late fees to their bills. Putting all that money from fees into your savings could mean a lovely family vacation or buying something for the home you've wished for. It could also be added to your retirement savings.

Getting rid of clutter will help to eliminate up to 40% of the housework you are dealing with, according to The National Soap and Detergent Association, based on the average home. In addition, decluttering and eliminating excess "stuff" you don't love or need can help reduce stress and create a calmer space and clearer head.

According to NAPO, the percentage of items we keep that are never used is very high, up to 80%. Finding a place in your home to store something doesn't mean you should keep it. How many of us, including me, have bought duplicate items because we couldn't find the one we had? That equals money out the window. If you have two things, you only require one, donate or sell the other. If it is hidden in the corner of a closet and you have no use for it, you will not notice it if it's gone.

Almost everyone has a cell phone. Using your smartphone and other organizational tools, such as your PC, MAC, or tablet, to track or plan your time may save you up to a 38% improvement in your home, according to Mobile Technology Products. You can use a notepad or a calendar if you are not tech-savvy. They help improve time management and remind you to pay bills on time by setting up notifications. You could also use a tickle file. We will explain that one later when we get to the home office. I could go on spouting statistics all day, but that is not the primary purpose of this book. Let's move on and check out our home the way it is now.

(See Appendix A for a list of more statistics).

Assessing the Present Condition

Take a realistic look around your home and be honest with yourself when you analyze the current state of each room and storage space. It can be tricky, to be honest with yourself, but honesty is what you need. Look for wasted spaces or spaces not currently used. I found things I didn't really care for or need and I found spaces wasted. Are you like me and tend to procrastinate in deciding what to keep or let go? Learning to clean up and put away for myself as I went was a challenge I had to overcome. However, discovering how much easier it is to do it as it comes up makes me very happy. It is always worth that tiny bit of extra time. I learned through this journey that not having those things hanging over my head, actually makes me smile.

Whatever issues or obstacles you are dealing with in this process, be assured I have dealt with them too. I piled, cluttered, and avoided deciding what to do with an item until I tossed it in a box, a drawer, or a closet to be dealt with later. It has led to chaos in my home, mind, and whole life. I have three grown daughters, and I am thankful that all of them learned from my flaws and are much better at staying organized than I have been.

Now they have inspired me to do better and make my home my happy place.

Writing this book has taught me a lot about my life and about my outlook on things. I don't need all the things I once thought I did. I can let go of much more than I ever dreamed I could, and I am happy about it. The people and experiences in my life are most important to me in the future, and even though some of the things are gone, I still have all the memories.

Do you tend to hoard certain things? I quilt so my item was fabric. Find a place to fold it up and keep it in then done. WRONG! I'm not sure how many quilts I thought I could make in one life time but I have enough fabric and more. That can be hard to conquer. I have started by not allowing myself to buy more until I have used some of what I have. It has tested my normal behavior and forced me to break some bad habits.

There was always something I had that I would hold in my hand and say to myself, I might need that someday, so let's just put it in a box or a drawer somewhere. It is usually very inexpensive and has a five percent chance that it will ever be needed again. Even if that occasion came up and I needed it, I most likely could not find it. Knowing what you need and where to find it is a great relief. If that ever happens, I have learned to let go and buy one when I need it.

Another thing that was not in my favor is that I tend to be a person of clutter and bad habits when it comes to housekeeping. Some don't mind housework at all and find it enjoyable. I don't just dislike it. I deplore it and will find anything else I can do to keep from doing it. With the clutter cleared and the time I've saved, I don't find it the struggle I once thought it was.

Now that you have taken an honest look at your situation, it's time to create just for you, a plan that fits your lifestyle and take action to change your home's current state of clutter and get more organized. Bring some calm and order to your life. I am so glad I did, and I think you will be too.

CREATE A PLAN TO FIT YOUR LIFE

There are many approaches to organizing your home. Some like the one-touch method, pick up an item once and decide about staying or going in that moment, then put it away or toss it but don't pick it up again to change your decision. Sorry, my brain doesn't function that fast for most things. But it might work for you.

You might be more successful with the method "The Life-Changing Magic of Tidying Up: The Japanese Art of Decluttering and Organizing ."(Kondo, 2014). Her book is very detailed and minimalist-inspired but can be relatively rigid when going through her process. The main principle is to hold everything in your hand for a few seconds, and if that something doesn't spark joy, get rid of it. I'm sorry, but some of those utensils in my kitchen don't spark joy, but I need them to make dinner for the family. Remove anything you don't need or use, even if it has sentimental value. This process is strict and overreaching, even in telling you how to fold your socks.

Then there is the Feng Shuai method, learn to arrange furniture and things in your home to bring balance and positive energy into your life.

My time and patience would have to be better for some of these methods. Still, they are philosophies many have used and are completely happy with. My advice may sound simple to some, but we need that bump in motivation or a guide to get started. Clean up your home, keep functional items, and keep a few meaningful things.

It's OK to save and touch that quilt Mom made for you from Grandma's sewing machine and find it a place to live in your home. Keep one of your child's favorite toys and clothes that hold cherished memories of the happy childhood you provided for them.

High school yearbooks might make you and your friends laugh together years later when you get together. I pull mine out and look at the pictures inside; they give me happy memories. Some of these things are part of you! It's not a crime to have some stuff. Don't live in a mess and let the property overtake your life. That's what happened to me. Have a clean and functional home.

The approach in this book is much more geared to your busy lifestyle. It requires fitting the process into your life rather than fitting your life around the method. You can still achieve your goals. It may take more time.

If you get burned out halfway through, and quit trying; you will never get the results you want. If doing one space or room at a time is better for you, keep in mind each small achievement adds up to significant results. <u>Done is always better than perfect!</u>

Here are some steps to take to get started coming up with the plan that works for you:

1. Grab a notepad or notebook and pen, and begin by writing down everything important to you and your family.

2. List every space in your home.

3. Get bags or boxes ready and labeled for trash, donate or sell, and relocate to a different area in the home.

4. This is a big job; to keep it less than overwhelming, break it down into smaller tasks.

5. Make a commitment to developing anti-clutter habits.

6. Set goals of what you want to achieve each week and enter them in your planner.

7. Include plans to maintain each area once organized, either weekly or by taking a short amount of time each day. Fifteen to thirty minutes a day works well for maintaining order.

I am sentimental and busy, and rushing doesn't always work. My life has been whole, and I have many things that bring a smile to my face, so I was somewhere outside the plans listed in the beginning of this chapter. Please review your lifestyle and determine the process that will work best for you. It gets easier and easier as you go. Create a plan and a schedule that fits your life.

Be realistic and do your best to stick to your schedule, knowing that emergencies or conflicts happen. When they do, be prepared to reassess your plan and keep going, don't give up. Doing it all in a week might be fantastic for some and overwhelming for others.

As we advance, you should lay out a plan that allows an allotted amount of time each day or week to reach your goals gradually. It would be best to do bits daily instead of feeling defeated with the full scope.

Every step you take will give you a feeling of achievement. The size of your home is also something you have to think about. If you live in a small apartment, you can achieve your goals in a much shorter time than someone living in a large two-story home.

Also, consider your family's willingness to help on this journey as a part of your plan. Engage them as much as possible because they will also reap the benefits of a more organized home.

After your assessment, please recognize the areas you want to improve that will have the most impact with the least effort. This helps keep you motivated for the bigger jobs to come. A daily planner will help keep you on track with your goals, and not only will your home become more organized, but your life will be more organized too. Put tasks to accomplish each day in the planner or calendar but don't put so many that you feel overwhelmed.

Keep in mind other appointments and responsibilities so that everything is covered. You can list those goals by room or storage space in your home, and you will know what is on your schedule each day. Make it fit your life and the amount of time you can dedicate to this endeavor, and be realistic in your goals. You will be surprised that you get more and more motivated once you start. After an area or two are done, you may even enjoy it. For example, I emptied and organized my desk drawer first. If all you do the first day is clean and declutter a junk drawer that only takes about fifteen minutes, that is a success!

I will include a link to some worksheets in the back of the book with what is included there and feel free to download and print it. You may prefer having a digital copy to work with and that too is available. Included is a checklist to get you started. It follows along with the book chapters and categories. Adjust it as you see fit, or follow along.

No rule demands you have to do them in the order listed. That's just my plan and it developed as I was working through the process. You may start with any room or area that bothers you the most. Enter them in your planner, organizer, or calendar(also included) to keep you on track.

Remember that even small wins are wins!

Check off each item on the list or mark it off in your planner as you finish it for an incredible feeling of self-satisfaction and accomplishment. As you go through your home and reap the benefits, it will encourage you to do more.

I feel a sense of relief each time I move an item out of my space and send it on it's way, whether it is a donation, sale or piece of trash. Maintaining order gets easier with each step.

Make a schedule or plan for maintenance as well. Maintaining each area becomes second nature once you cut down on the clutter and will feel much less like something to avoid.

Declutter Then Organize Room by Room

Allowing clutter to accumulate in your home is just avoiding deciding what to do with an item. If you use it, keep it. If you love it, preserve and display it. If you have a place to store it, time or resources to maintain it, keep it. Otherwise, it adds to the chaos, and the item should go.

We will go through a process here to declutter rooms and spaces that are typically a problem to deal with and that we try to avoid. First, we will sort all the items, get rid of the clutter, clean the area, and then get it organized in a way to make it easier to maintain.

Much of this chapter will be based on my own experience with my clutter and the research I have done.

Depending on the amount of clutter in your home, this process may take little time or be very time-consuming. It will be challenging at times to focus and stay motivated, but the pointers and tips here will help you attack the problem at your own pace and try to follow the plan you have laid out in your planner or calendar.

I promise that if you stay the course and keep at it bit by bit each day, it will make a massive difference in how you feel about yourself and your home, giving you a sense of achievement. You will be amazed at the difference it can make for you and your family.

As you go through each space, categorize your items. You should have four boxes or bags ready before beginning and label each. You will have one each for donations, sales, moving to a more appropriate place, and trash.

This sorting makes the job much easier. Once you make a decision, stick with it. Don't overthink it. Your first instinct is usually right. It doesn't matter if you use boxes or bags, but please be sure to label each one. After making the decision, clean the surfaces. Put the items neatly back in an organized fashion if they belong in the area and move on to the next space or room. This is basic to each area and I sometimes repeat this for each just to keep you on track.

When you fill the donation or sell box, remove it from the area so you are not tempted to second-guess yourself and pull items back out. Putting the donation items in the car immediately for dropping them off keeps me from doing just that. I donate almost everything and sell very little because that works best for me.

If selling works for you, you should set aside an area in the garage or a shed to store items until sale day.

We will also cover some items or tools to help you organize and maintain your spaces. Some will be low-cost, and some will be made up of things you already have. Small dividers or containers can help in drawers. Shelf dividers help make the most of closet or kitchen shelves.

Baskets for laundry in each bedroom help round up the piles of clothes, making your laundry day much more efficient. Some suggestions will require a purchase, and some will not. You should do it in a way that suits the budget you are working with. In the future a good rule of thumb to follow is when you buy a new item, discard an item to keep clutter at bay.

Room by Room, Space by Space, Here we go!!!

Tackling Junk Drawers

I started small with these drawers where all kinds of things accumulate and seem to magically multiply. We all have at least one junk drawer in the kitchen, bathroom, or desk. I have 4 in my kitchen alone and I won't even mention how many duplicated items I found.

First, take everything out of the drawer and wipe it clean. Then, put things back in an organized fashion, but only items that belong in that space and are convenient for you there. Organizing similar items together makes them easier to find and takes less time to keep tidy.

It is entirely up to you if you use small organizers or place your items loosely in the drawer.

Don't pack containers in the drawer too closely if you use containers. That way, your eye will go directly to the item you're looking for. Also, combine similar items to make the most of those drawers. It may depend on the types of items you keep in the drawer and whether you use any containers or dividers.

Consider using a silverware organizer to divide up the space. I have them in my desk drawer to organize pens, pencils, and markers. Some small containers are even adjustable for a very customized space.

You should go through these every couple of months and ensure only items that belong there are there. If things are placed back after use, they will stay in good order requiring very little time to maintain that order.

The key is to eliminate things you have had no use for in a very long time or that you have forgotten you had. I found that I had several duplicate items that I could get rid of too. Donate or sell any of those items. That's it.

If you have multiple junk drawers, move on to the next one and follow the same process. Now when you open that drawer, your things will be where they belong, and it will already simplify your life and put a smile on your face. You would only need ten to fifteen minutes per drawer, and you will already feel a sense of achievement. Good start.

Success!

Home Office

My desk was one of my priorities, so that was at the top of my list, and while I was there, I decided to work on putting the home office in order too. Always loose papers floating around, a collection of glasses or cups, and other assorted items that don't even belong there.

The books were in a jumble and the shelves in a mess. So much time lost looking for a pencil or pad of paper, not to mention those pesky bills that need paying before late charges are added.

The result of my organized office is this book and the inspiration to keep writing.

I started with the desk since having a friendly, neat workspace gives me pleasure and makes me more productive.

For the surface, take everything off and wipe it down. My desktop is laminate, so I used spray cleaner and a rag or paper towel to wipe it all down while it was empty. I'll keep the bags or boxes handy because there will be lots of trash and donations here to get rid of.

Right now, I have vitamins(move to the bathroom), coffee, an empty glass (goes to the kitchen), an extra snack to relocate, and a stack of papers that we will group with any found in other parts of the house. That task can be done while watching TV, listening to music, or audiobooks.

There is a nest of messy cables that need some attention. The cords and cables are necessary, but use some cable clips or twist ties to corral them into some semblance of order.

Now I put my computer back along with a notepad; of course, pens and pencils will reside in one of the drawers. I have a lamp and only one picture frame(digital), so I can enjoy my children and grandchildren while I work.

In the introduction, I said I would explain a tickler file and how it can help keep you on target. A tickler file is a system for organizing reminders and essential documents by date. It's often a physical folder or accordion file with pockets or sections labeled by month or day.

Each document or task is filed according to its due date or deadline. Tickler files are commonly used in businesses and offices to keep track of ongoing projects, delegated tasks, and important dates such as meetings, appointments, and deadlines.

They can also be used for personal organization, such as keeping track of bills to save on late fees or other important dates. When you file something in the tickler file, you'll be reminded of it on the day it's due or a few days before, so you have enough time to prepare. This can help prevent missed deadlines, forgotten tasks, and other problems from poor time management.

If you would prefer, you can use the calendar or spreadsheet on your PC to keep track of dates and set reminders. This can eliminate a lot of paper hanging around in the way.

If you didn't clean out your desk drawers with the junk drawers, now is the time to empty them, wipe them out, and only put items there that will be useful at the desk.

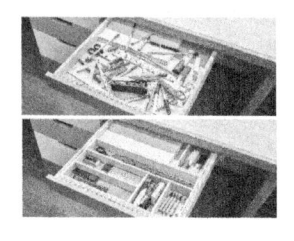

Next, take things off the shelves and wipe them down. Sort your books, pictures, and small items you want to keep and put them back in an eye pleasing fashion. Discard the rest or move them to their proper place.

File drawers and cabinets can be grouped with paper when you get ready to do that. You can sweep your floor after ridding the room of clutter and move on. That wasn't so hard, was it?

Great job!

Hallways

It was a small area, so I found the Hallway one of the most effortless spaces to clear in my home. Most people come into the hall and set down whatever they have in their hands. Please find a way to get family members and yourself to put things away before putting them down.

Ensure space is designated for shoes, backpacks, purses, and hats. A hall or coat closet can double for these items. By the way, bribery works with family. If they do it for a month, take them out for ice cream or their favorite treat. I have read it should only take twenty-one days to form or break a habit. The same ritual as before applies here. Keep the bags or boxes ready and labeled.

Empty the hall and only put back what you want or need there. For instance, we had a hat rack with some hats no one ever wore. Get rid of those, so there is room for those you like and use on the stand. A small table with a bowl to toss keys and change in when entering the front door keeps small items together.

Clean the floor while the hall is empty. Hang a nice picture on your wall and only put functional or multifunctional furniture back. If you have more than one hall, following the same process, keeping in mind that halls in different parts of the house serve other purposes. The primary function they have in common is to travel from one area in the house to another. Check this one off the list as another success.

Neat is nice!

Living Room/Family Room

One room, which is one of the most challenging rooms to keep neat and organized, is also one of the busiest rooms in your home. It is your living room or family room.

Having things lined up on your coffee table in neat rows does not necessarily mean you are organized. If you have a table full of magazines, determine if you will read them. Are they pleasing to the eye? Should you instead put them in a magazine rack? Keep them for a month; toss them if you haven't read them or some senior citizen homes would love to have them. Could you cancel those subscriptions if you have collected them for several months without reading them? Money saved!

Are the things on your tables things you love looking at? Are they used in this room? You can put all the remote controls in a nice basket or decorative box on the table for a more organized look. A tricky part of this process is being frank with yourself when answering these questions.

You might have a knickknack there, and if you love it, keep it there; if not, let it go. Putting like items in small collections of three add interest and makes it look nice.

Could you take a quick mental inventory of the space? Too many throw pillows can be viewed as clutter. Only have one or two for a cleaner feel. You may like rotating them seasonally or just a change instead of having them all out at once. An area can be brightened by changing worn rugs for a fresher look.

Too much furniture in a room can also give it a cluttered feel. You also want to keep in mind that you need seating for yourself and your guests. Try rearranging first to see if that makes it look and feel better to you. If not, remove a piece or two. If that works, you can relocate those to another place, donate or sell them.

Empty all your tables and shelves and categorize the items in the same method. Put back only the things you love, or that have great sentimental value to you and those you use in this space. Set up a charging station to hide your phone or tablet and cables. A small basket works well for this.

A large basket in the corner can hold a couple of blankets when the temperature drops, or when you like to cuddle up with a good book on the sofa. An ottoman that opens is also a good place for those blankets.

Have an attractive bowl or a box to put remote controls in on your end table rather than have them scattered around. Decorative boxes on a shelf work to hide those small items you might need in the room. Relocate all the others unless they are to toss, donate or sell.

Clutter will inevitably work its way back into the room. Be prepared. Have a small basket or container in an out-of-the-way spot to catch that clutter when it comes, using it as a temporary solution. Keep it small so that too much doesn't come in. Go through and empty that container when it gets full and put them all back where they belong or dispose of them.

Once you have achieved success here, I hope when you enter the room you feel calm and happy!

Kitchen

We've taken care of the junk drawers, and we hope it is still working for you and has significantly reduced the time spent looking for things. remember that you should go through them now and then to make sure only the items you want there are the items that belong. Now we must organize our counters, cabinets, other drawers, the refrigerator, and the pantry. We know we can conquer it because we have already come so far.

Beginning with the rest of the drawers in the kitchen, let's check out that silverware drawer first. Consider buying an inexpensive divider if your knives, forks, and spoons are thrown loosely in a drawer. Having each one in its compartment will be easier to find and put away. I also have a knife drawer. Get a divider for those if you have knives in assorted sizes for different uses. For example, you have steak, bread, and carving knives. They can all have their own space. It looks much nicer, and you are less likely to end up with cuts and scratches on your fingers and hands.

Next, you have a drawer for spatulas, ladles, and serving ware. Again, if you want dividers or to have those loose large pieces in the drawer, it's entirely your preference. Remember to keep like items together to avoid duplication and wasted space. Many people keep them in a nice container on the counter or have a place on the wall to hang them. Whatever works best for your kitchen should be your choice. Be sure that as you progress, you have emptied and wiped out each drawer as you go.

The biggest job you will do in this room is organizing your cabinets. Where should I keep the glasses, cups, dishes, and cookware? I like to keep the item closest to where they will be used. For example, glasses are more convenient in a cabinet by the sink. You can store Cups and mugs close to your coffee pot or teapot. Dishes and china close to the table where you use it. All this sounds like common sense, but we don't know how or why things get shuffled around sometimes but they do.

Let's start with that cabinet under the sink that always seems to be a mess where things are hard to find when needed. Begin again by taking everything out and wiping it all down. You could even put a small motion sensor light under there to keep it from feeling dingy and help you find or replace things. One great idea is to put a tension rod in and hang all those spray bottles you have in there on it. They are up higher and more visible. If they are too heavy for a tension rod, you can always use the screw in kind. To get those trash bags out more quickly, hang a short curtain rod on the cabinet door and put the roll of trash bags on it. That makes it easy to unroll one and tear it off without digging around in the box. Another idea is to stack a couple of wine bins under there and store trash bags in them on the rolls. We all usually have more than one size of a trash bag. Screwing a couple of plastic containers to the door is a great place to keep sponges and scrubbers so they aren't hanging around the sink. You can use a few clear plastic bins for all the other little things you store there.

We already took care of the drawers. That includes those junk drawers we all have. Take the time once a month to review them again to ensure they stay organized. Now it should only take a couple of minutes. We did the hard part earlier. Now and then, when doing dishes, you could empty a drawer and wipe it out to keep it clean.

Countertops

Now we will work on the organization of our counters. When I began this journey, my counters were cluttered with many things that did not belong there. I had food containers and small appliances that were rarely used. They needed a new home out of sight, but things we never use should go in the donation or sell pile. When I start on the pantry, those we keep will live there until needed. I am a coffee addict, so moving the coffeepot is not even a consideration. A microwave and a convection oven take up lots of room, but moving them to another location would be impractical. I do have three sets of canisters on the counter that should be pared down to one set, depending on what is stored in them..

Next in line in my kitchen is the refrigerator. I had a couple of "science projects" growing in there, and who knows how old they might have been. :))) Get rid of those and any other condiments and foods way past their expiration dates. I had my trash bag nearby for that.

Just doing that much freed up lots of space for the good stuff. As we have before, take everything out. Wipe down the shelves and wash out the bins or drawers. We are off to a great start here. Take verbal or physical notes on paper of the things you tossed that need replacing. Put items back in the most convenient spaces to you or their designated spots. Put like items near each other or sort by how you will use them together. When you open that door now, everything is bright, clean, and organized. That was a big job, so give yourself a treat and a pat on the back. If you have come this far, be very proud of your success!

Pantry

Keeping your pantry clutter-free will make finding what you need when you need it easier. This can also help to maximize your storage space. If you are lucky and have a pantry, many homes don't. In that case, you know how odd items can accumulate there over time. Keeping organized can be challenging because every household member has access.

You will need those bags or boxes for trash, relocate and donate. In this instance, the donations will go to a food bank. I would attack the pantry differently and do one shelf at a time. If you have the time, empty it entirely and lay everything on the table, counter, or floor. To begin organizing your pantry in the most effective way, take everything out. If you skip corners now and only remove a portion of the items, this will result in a less organized system and more effort in the long run. Wipe down the shelves, and if you like having a shelf liner, then put them in.

Sort the items you removed into categories and decide what you want to keep. For those you will keep, put like items in groups so when you put them back, you have canned items, baking supplies, kids' snacks, and cereals all grouped together on the shelves so they are easy to locate. Group them based on your family's needs. Put the oldest use-by date in front of newer items of the same kind. That way, they won't be wasted. Put newer items that are the same to the back. Check the best-used-by dates for any food item you have that no one in the house will eat (not sure where those come from). Anything past their best-used-by dates will go straight into the trash. If they still pass that check, then put them in donations. Very simple but can take a bit of time.

Food in bulky cardboard boxes takes up too much space and adds clutter to your pantry. Instead, remove food from its original packaging and put it inside clear storage containers instead. You can find low-cost containers at most stores, and depending on your budget, you can buy plastic or glass as long as they have lids. This will allow you to see the contents and know when it's time to put it on your next grocery list.

This makes it easier to create areas in your pantry for specific foods. You can easily remove a single container to find what you need instead of searching through an entire shelf.

A nice thing but not a necessity to have would be an inventory posted on the inside of the pantry door. You can cross items off as they are used, and add them to the grocery list for your next shopping order. You could also use a small whiteboard and dry-erase marker to track if that works better for you. another option for keeping up with inventory is to paint the back of the pantry door with chalkboard paint with a place near it for chalk. That would be quick and easy. An app on your phone is a convenient way to keep an updated grocery list. It is always with you; you can add items on the go.

Laundry Room

My laundry room is relatively small compared to others I have seen. Start with clearing out all the things that are left out on top of the washer and dryer. If you have cabinets above them, empty them as well. Wipe down all the surfaces and while everything is out in the open, take an inventory of all your items. This is the perfect time to add anything running low on your shopping list. If you like keeping basics on the washer or dryer for convenience, that is your choice. Extras or items infrequently used can be stored in the cabinets or your pantry.

Visual clutter actively works against any efforts to create a serene space. Think of busy labels, mismatched containers, and packaging. Little changes like taking fresh dryer sheets from their blaring package and putting them into a lovely tissue holder make a laundry room calm, intentional, and aesthetically pleasing. You can empty liquid detergents, softeners, and wool dryer balls into glass jars. Once that is done, labeling things may be something you think is unnecessary. It is a tremendously clever way to help you stay organized. When everything has a clear, designated space, then things stay tidy. Then everybody in your household can see where everything goes at a glance. , if you don't want to be troubled with putting things in new containers, another way to attack visual clutter is to organize items in bins. Put like items together, one for detergents and fabric softeners, general cleaning products, and dryer sheets.

If working with limited space, make sure you maximize what you have. Walls are often not used at all, and there are many ways to use them. Storing items like irons, drying racks, brooms, or mops on the wall via hooks or tracks. When things are stored on the walls and off the ground, it leads to less clutter. If you have enough room, incorporate "clothes to put away" baskets for everyone. You can hand off clean clothes to each family member to put away and then return them to the laundry room for the next batch.

Make the space feel as comfortable and inviting as possible since laundry is probably not your favorite thing to do. Consider making a goal to wipe surfaces and mop the area once a week while doing laundry. Details, beautiful and functional, will dress up the space while still being user-friendly. If you start with a pleasing and functional space, you will develop a routine to maintain order.

Bedroom Closets

For most of us, closets might be one of our biggest challenges. It certainly is for me. Mine had stacks of boxes, extra blankets and pillows, and who knows what else. So many things just get tucked away in the corner and forgotten.

The first step for your closet is to take everything out. Everything! That includes things on the shelves, hanging items, and everything on the floor. Of course, if you want to do a bit at a time that fits your schedule, you can do that too. However, starting with an empty space is a great way get it right the first time. It sounds harder that way, but in the end, you will be much happier with the result. If you only have to go through this one time thoroughly, after that, it is easier and takes a reduced amount of time to maintain.

If you decide it better fits your schedule to do parts now and then, keep the parts you have finished, organized. Here is a hint, if you need help with your wardrobe letting things go. Take all your hanging clothes off the rack and turn them backward. When you wear or wash an item, put it at the front facing you when you hang it back up. Set a date in three to six months to take another look. Any items still facing the wrong direction will give you a good idea that you no longer need or use that item. Let it go and free up some space.

I think shelf dividers may be helpful depending on what you store on the shelves. For example, I have more oversized items on my shelves, such as blankets and extra pillows for guests.

Therefore, dividers are optional for those or completely unnecessary.

I recommend devoting a whole day to your closet. I am also listing closets before bedrooms because emptying the closet will fill the bedroom with stuff. Also, doing the bedroom first could tempt you to take a shortcut and stuff things in that closet to make the bedroom look neat and organized. Doing the closet first will help you avoid that temptation. What are all those boxes stacked in the corner? How long have they been packed away? Do you even know what you have in them anymore? Time to unpack them and make some choices on what stays or goes.

Be mindful as you put things back in the closet. Organizing clothes in a closet is essential for maintaining an orderly and efficient wardrobe. A systematic approach can make a significant difference when it comes to hanging clothes. Sort your garments by category, such as shirts, dresses, jackets, and pants.

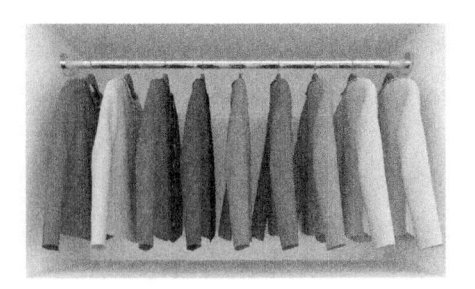

Within each category, further organize them by color or occasion, depending on your preference. This arrangement allows for easy visual identification and quick access to specific items.

To maximize space, invest in high-quality hangers that match the clothing type. Padded or velvet hangers prevent clothes from slipping off, while slimline hangers create extra room for more garments. Choose your favorites.

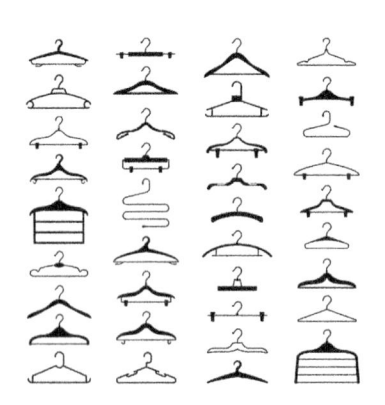

Start by hanging longer items like dresses and coats towards the back of the closet, as they require more vertical space.

Shorter items like shirts and blouses can be arranged towards the front. Next, place the garments Within each category from light to dark shades or casual to formal, ensuring a visually pleasing and streamlined display. Finally, consider leaving space between each item to prevent overcrowding and wrinkling.

Additionally, group clothing sets or outfits makes getting dressed a breeze. Finally, use additional storage accessories like hanging organizers, hooks, or cascading hangers for scarves, belts, or ties. Following these guidelines will make your closet a well-organized space, allowing you to quickly find and maintain your clothing collection.

Another way to get things up off the floor or easy to access is to put hooks on the inside of the closet door. You could also install a small curtain rod to hang small items. The closet should look neat and organized now with the clutter and unused items gone and everything where it belongs.

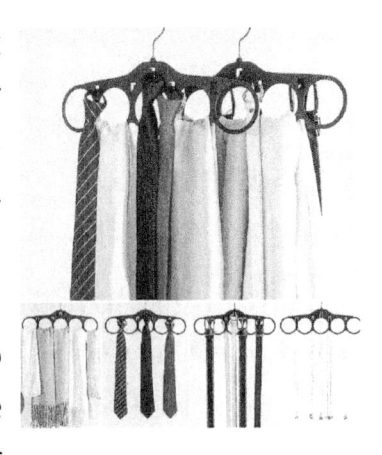

Give yourself a gold star!

Bedrooms

As in all other spaces, begin by decluttering. That statement is repetitive but essential, makes things move faster and keeps you on track. Get the bags and boxes ready once again, and let's go!

Studies show that an organized and tidy area will aid your sleep and elevate your mood when getting up. Think about how you feel when staying in a nice hotel room. I love waking up in that nice space and not having so much "stuff" around me.

Good organization and plentiful storage is the key in the bedroom. A cluttered area adds to the stress and makes it harder to relax. Please don't get overwhelmed because it can be a big job. Mine was quite stressful and a hard place to let go of some of my things.

Start small and begin with something as simple as jewelry or your bedside table. You may have a nice jewelry box to store the items you want to keep, or you can also put small organizers in a drawer to keep things needed and easily accessible.

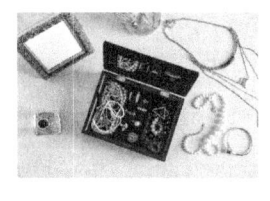

As you go, ask yourself if the item is functional and does what it's supposed to do or does it look good in the space and makes you happy. When you finish each job, stop and give yourself a treat—a piece of chocolate or a nice cup of tea. Complete one area at a time and take time to enjoy your progress. You aim to create a calm and restful room that can be your happy space for quiet moments.

Making your bed every morning is a good beginning if that is not a habit you already have. With the bed made, it already gives you a sense of accomplishment, and your day has barely begun. "Wake and Make." Marines start the day with this simple task. "Make Your Bed: Little Things That Can Change Your Life . . . and Maybe the World," a book on the #1 New York Times bestseller of powerful life lessons. . by retired Navy Adm. William H. McRaven. This was also presented as a Navy SEAL's inspiring graduation speech on May 17, 2014.

Now you can tackle surfaces one at a time. You have nightstands, a dresser, and a chest of drawers. That is a typical bedroom. Take each one at a time. Go through all the items you have there. Labeled bags and boxes at hand to sort as you go until the top of that surface is empty. Wipe down and put the things back that belong and only what belongs.

My nightstand gets full of items I don't need there, so there was a lot of relocation for things like lotion, snacks, and magazines I've read. I needed a lamp and a charger for my phone and tablet. Some nightstands come with a USB connections in the top drawer to keep things neat. So much nicer now.

Think about storage. The better your storage ideas, the easier to maintain an uncluttered and organized space. Some of this may depend upon the budget you have.

I love having a chair and stool in my bedroom. It looks stylish and if you add a small table and stool, it provides a cozy space for reading or a cup of coffee when you need some alone time. In picking a stool, I like one that opens where I can stash a lap quilt or small blanket. Another option would be putting a bench at the foot of the bed. Some open up for more storage or have open shelves underneath for baskets or books.

What about the bed? Under the bed is an excellent place often forgotten about when it comes to storage. It can hold extra pillows or blankets.

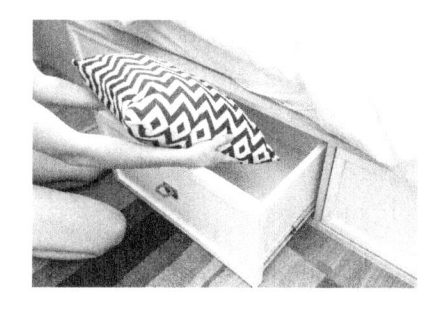

It could also be used for out-of-season clothes that can be kept in plastic bins. Some bins come with rollers, so they pull out for easy access.

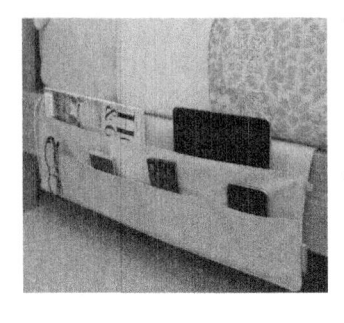

You could also use a bedside compartmented hanger for keeping the TV remote, your latest favorite magazine, reading glasses, and your phone or tablet reader in.

The largest surface in the bedroom is the dresser. I don't know about you, but mine accumulates many things that don't belong. It's too easy to walk by and lay down whatever you have in your hand, get distracted, and then walk away. Soon you have a mess you want to avoid looking at or dealing with. You must also remember what's there causing you to spend too much time looking for things where they don't belong. A candle or perhaps even your jewelry box can be nice, but very little else. A small group of knick-knacks works but can start to look cluttered again if there are too many. It also takes longer to clean. Pick two or three pieces you love and send the rest to live somewhere else.

Next would be your chest of drawers. Mine has a TV on it and only a little else, but otherwise, it would be as piled up as the dresser. Take off everything that's not useful or beautiful to look at. Wipe it down. Stand back and enjoy the work you have put in.

Drawers are next. Empty the drawers of everything, even if you only do one drawer a day, and categorize in your bags or boxes and put back only the things you use or are helpful.

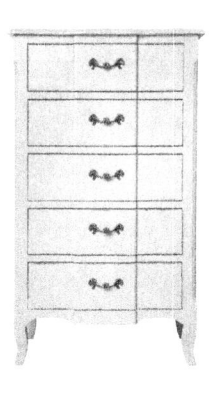

Sort things you are keeping into categories and keep like items together. Your number of drawers will determine the number of categories in each drawer. Use dividers in drawers to keep small items like socks or lingerie and make it easy when putting away laundry and knowing what goes where and where to find what you need, thus saving you more time for yourself. Nightstands or bedside tables with drawers can increase storage a lot, but again, only put what belongs in the space and you use when going to bed or getting up. You can also have a table without drawers. There, you can use lidded boxes or baskets to neaten up.

Your bedroom now should be a place that calms you down and brings you joy.

You may be amazed, as I was, at all the things you had forgotten about, collected in corners. If you don't remember you had it, you probably don't need to keep it, or it needs to live in a different place in your home. Let go of the rest, and when you open those drawers, you can find what you're looking for without searching. More time saved!

Guest Room

Many things that apply to your bedroom can also be used in your guest room. Having guests in your home can be enjoyable, and making them feel welcome and comfortable matters to you. Have a place for their suitcase during their stay. Provide a clock, a calendar, and a lamp for reading. Also, share the login information for your Wi-Fi connection. They might appreciate a full-length mirror nearby, even if it is in the hall or bath.

Perhaps they would like to have a TV in the room. So they don't have to get up once settled in, make sure the remote is near the bed so they can easily change channels or adjust the volume. If they use a computer during their visit, provide a small table near an internet connection or power outlet. Provide pens, pencils, and paper. If they like to write home during their stay, ensure they have stamps and envelopes though most use email now.

If they are going out, offer them a key to your home so they have access if you are away or sleeping when they return. If you have a security system providing the code they need to reenter. I think providing maps could be helpful, and you can use a highlighter to mark places of interest. If they use GPS to navigate the area, give them a list of addresses of the best shopping areas, restaurants, parks, and museums nearby.

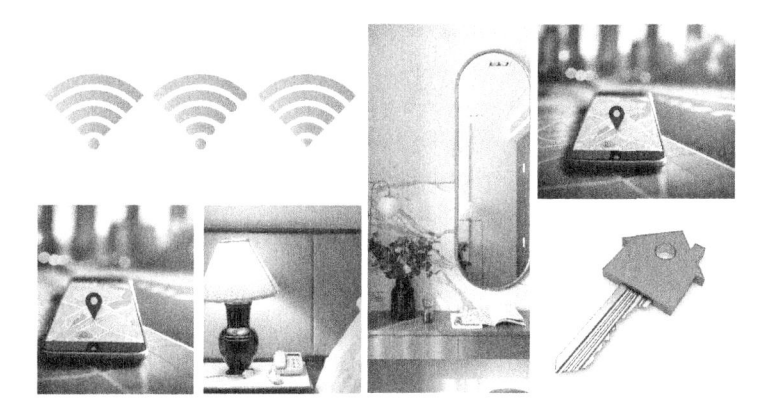

The bed should be comfortable, and the linens should be the best quality your budget will allow. Keep an extra set on hand. If you can't afford a quality mattress, use a quality air mattress on top of the box springs. Some of them are very comfortable. Please provide them with a choice of pillows and a comforter. An extra super cuddly blanket at the foot of the bed would also be nice. Make sure you have window coverings so they have privacy. If you want a low-cost solution, just put a shade up.

This room can double as extra storage for out-of-season clothes but ensure space for guests to put away their things. Over-the-door hangers or hooks inside the closet door can provide them a place for a robe, purse, or coat.

Leave them a couple of empty drawers and several hangers to use. You might put a basket on the dresser for small items they may have forgotten, such as lotions and soaps. That will give your guest access to them if needed. Another small bowl or basket can be left empty for guests' small belongings. Current magazines on a nightstand or magazine rack might also be welcoming. That will give your guest access to them if needed.

Don't fool yourself that you can put any items in that room that you have yet to decide about keeping or going. If you do, you will end up with too many things to deal with later. Being disciplined and keeping your guest room neat should be simple once it's in order. When you don't have guests, you might find the room a calm and comfortable place to escape.

Bathrooms

No matter what size your bathroom is, it can be organized. A small bathroom can be a bit more challenging, but it can be done. You can be creative and pack a lot of utility into a tiny space. It requires having a place for toilet paper, towels, and things like toothbrushes and, at the same time, keeping them looking neat. Various containers can be used to keep like items together and easily accessible. We will provide some ideas to maximize space in a small bathroom and give you some ideas for a larger bathroom.

One way to add storage is to add shelves above the toilet. Shelves for this may be purchased or made, depending on your budget. You can place baskets or jars there to keep items in order, and they look lovely. Clear containers under the sink can be a way of keeping it neat and things easy to find. The containers you use can be sizes tailored to your needs and are relatively inexpensive. If you like, labels can be added. These are useful, but using a fun font to print them also makes them attractive. On top of the vanity, add a small tray to keep things together that you like having handy. That might include hand soap, lotion, and sanitizer.

You can add a multi-level storage unit if you have extra floor space. Put things on the top you use most often and items like extra toilet paper and toiletries on the lower shelf. If you get a unit with rollers, you can quickly move it to where you need it or clean the floor in that area.

To give that tub or shower surround a clean, updated feel, and you can buy inexpensive shampoo, conditioner, and body wash dispensers that match and label them. It just gives a professionally organized bathroom look on a budget.

For those vanity drawers, you can refer to your junk drawer process. Don't keep things you don't use there, or you have another junk drawer instead of the organized space you want to create. Instead, add dividers so that everything frequently used has a spot. Put those items closer to the front for convenience and lesser-used items to the back of the drawer. If your cabinet has the space, you can also attach small baskets inside the doors to give easy access.

A space is needed for clean and dirty towels. If your linen closet is not in the bath, you can use baskets or buy a decorative hamper for the used towels and wash clothes. Extra clean towels can also be hung on towel racks. Something that can be very stylish is putting a small ladder leaning against the wall for extras. Adding a cabinet is another option for extra items if you have a large bath.

If you have small children, keep their bath toys in a waterproof container when they are not using them. That's one more way to keep them confined and out of the way. Be sure to clean them all frequently to avoid mold and mildew. Use some vinegar and baking soda if you are like me and hate the smell of bleach.

It shouldn't be hard to maintain when your bath is organized, functional, and comfortable. Of course, it will require a little work occasionally, but it will take much less time than it previously did. Put things back in place after use, and don't let them accumulate. It will become a small part of your daily routine rather than the massive cleaning you previously dealt with.

CHILDREN'S BEDROOMS AND PLAYROOMS

Follow the same steps in children's that applied to bedrooms with a few added suggestions. If you have children, have them go through their collection of toys and sort out the ones they frequently play with. Toys and stuffed animals accumulate fast, so this should be repeated often. If there is no home for an item, determine if it is meaningful to the child. If it is, find it a home or convince them to give it up. Children's beds sometimes come with drawers underneath. They are easy for a child to reach and might eliminate the need for a dresser. This could give the child more room to play.

Most children have books. Make sure they have simple storage for those and workbooks. Baskets or a spice rack attached to the wall can be a great place to store books. You can even make a bookshelf with a short length of rain gutter.

When they get a new toy, teach them to donate or sell a toy to make room. This will guide them to be charitable and show how good it feels to pass toys on to shelters or homes where the children have few toys. Or sell them to know how earning a bit of money feels. It makes it easy to find the toy they want when they want it if they know where their toys are kept. That eliminates some of the complaining and whining, and they have eliminated some clutter and unwanted things. They will get much more enjoyment from the space.

BONUS!

Clean the surfaces and place the child's favorite things on display. Another place to display treasured items they love to see but don't play with might be a shelf above a window or door. Make it a game and offer a reward if they consistently pick up and put away without being told for a set amount of time, say a week. This teaches them organizational skills.

Another way to organize small items and get them off the floor is to use over-the-door shoe storage. It works great for dolls, doll clothes, boxes of markers, crayons, or pencils. Get the clear ones; they can easily see and find what they want to play with.

Shelves with buckets or baskets are great for building blocks or those army men or dinosaurs that boys love and for little girls who love bows and headbands. A hanging jewelry organizer on the back of the closet door provides great storage for small items. Another idea is to use some small organizers in a drawer and sort them there.

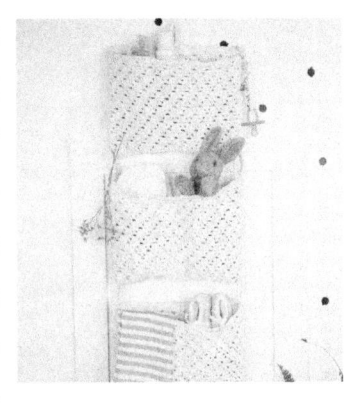

Some toys work well hung on a pegboard. Everything you can get up off the floor, the better. The kids will also like that because it gives them more play space.

A large basket or a toy box is great for odds and ends, but it can be hard for them to sort through and find what they want without emptying it all on the floor. Having some throw pillows on the bed might encourage them to curl up and read a book if it is so comfy. We love when they enjoy reading.

Winner again!

Linen, Coat, and Hall Closets

In our journey of understanding the elements of organized and harmonious living spaces, we have navigated through numerous areas of the home, deciphering the beauty and purpose of each one. In this chapter, we will delve into a part of the house that is too often overlooked yet is central to maintaining an orderly and comfortable living environment - the linen, hall, and coat closets.

These closets may seem mundane and inconsequential in interior design and home organization. They are not flashy, showy spaces like the living room or the kitchen that are immediately noticeable and consistently used. Yet, in these unseen spaces, these hidden compartments of our homes, we often find the true foundation of our day-to-day comfort and ease.

This chapter will explore the often underappreciated importance of linen, hall, and coat closets. We will navigate their uses to maximize their functionality.

Whether elegantly arranging towels and bed linens, strategically organizing your daily essentials, or efficiently storing your coats and outerwear, these closets can enhance the flow of your home life.

Moreover, we will uncover design and organization strategies to ensure these spaces are practical and aesthetically pleasing.

Properly managed closets contribute to the organization and the overall feel of the home, reflecting the care and thoughtfulness invested in every corner.

Ready your measuring tapes and notepads as we embark on a transformative journey from chaos to order, overlooked to celebrated, and from merely functional to beautifully efficient. Welcome to the world of linen, hall, and coat closets. I bet these closets can use some attention too. Once again, have your labeled bags or boxes ready.

Do you have linens that no longer fit the beds you have? Do you have too many towels? Women or Children's shelters Would probably be very happy to receive those things if they are in good condition.

Linen Closets

Using shelf dividers helps keep towels and wash clothes in order. Wash cloths can also be rolled up and stored in a row in a plastic container, basket, or even a shoe box. Whatever better fits your budget to keep them tidy. What about those wadded-up sheet sets? To make your shelf look nice and neat, fold them up and place each matched set together by putting the sheets inside the pillowcase. Then, when you're ready to make the bed, the entire set is together and ready. No digging around to find the ones that match.

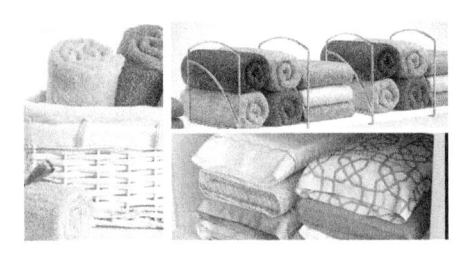

Time saved!

Coat/Hall Closets

What about coats that have been outgrown or that no one uses? If your coat closet is jam-packed, pull those out and either donate or sell them. Plenty of shelters would love to have them to pass out on cold days and nights. Some churches accept those types of donations, or if you are inclined. If any are tattered and worn down, toss them or use parts for pet bedding. Animal shelters use them for that reason as well.

We have yet to mention our hall closet. To start organizing a hall or entryway closet, Review all the bags, bins, and shelves to eliminate clutter or unused items. That could always use some TLC. It could be your coat closet, too, but it may be doing double duty as a place for sports equipment, hats, keys, or shoes. All the items should be easy to find and put away for the owner. If you keep shoes there, you can invest in an inexpensive shoe rack for a temporary storage solution when you kick off your shoes near the door. You might even use a very low shelf on the floor for two storage levels. A mirror inside the closet door will give you a last-minute check before leaving. If you have other hall closets away from the entry, think about the purpose you want them to serve and things you should keep close at hand for those areas.

Cleaning Closet

Do you have a closet somewhere with cleaning supplies? I do, and it has not been sorted out for years. Is there a broken vacuum or smelly old rags there? How many brooms do you need, and do they have broken handles? Toss them and start over. The house in that area will smell fresher, and you can gain extra storage, too, if needed.

I hope, at this point, you are feeling the advantages of living with less clutter. Whether you are following the outline or setting your own schedule, you are doing great and should be finding things much more efficiently than before, and as a bonus, you have saved a bit of money and time. Adding small hooks on the walls near or on the door offers a great place to hang your keys and other small items you need to grab on your way out.

Great work!

Papers and Digital Information

This topic encompasses so much that I have given it its own chapter. First, we will list each paper document you should keep and file away and the optional things. Some information can be scanned into a digital format; we will also cover that. Once we get through the papers, we will be ready to gather all photos and deal with them one at a time. Photos are your memories; I know how precious mine are to me. I have learned to let go of many along the way. They are damaged beyond repair, or I don't know who they are.

Paper clutter, just like regular household clutter, can cause significant STRESS. Yes, it's been scientifically proven by researchers at UCLA. Women, especially, are susceptible to higher stress levels if they live in a cluttered environment.

The amount of paperwork around your house can seem overwhelming. Mail keeps coming in and piling up. We get catalogs. Magazines, letters, newspapers, financial statements, tax documents, etc.

What to keep and what should go. Will I even read that paper or magazine? What documents are important enough to file? We are all dealing with information overload.

Let's get a grip on this and make it a manageable amount to handle.

To alleviate some of this:

1. Please get rid of junk mail as soon as it arrives. If you read the papers and magazines in a month, have a home for them, and at the end of the month, let them go.

2. If you never read them, save yourself some money and cancel those subscriptions.

3. Take a picture with your phone or scan any information you want to remember into your computer documents files.

This is a great way to keep up with announcements and invitations. I also do one of these with business cards I need so that they can be tossed.

Now let's break down the categories of what to keep and for how long.

Keep it in Your Wallet or Purse at all Times

- Driver's License or ID card
- Health Insurance card
- Medicare card unless it has your Social Security Number on it
- Your Blood type and Organ Donor Card
- Credit Cards and Debit Cards
- NEVER carry your Social Security Card

Keep Indefinitely

- Birth Certificates
- death Certificates
- marriage Certificates
- Social Security Cards
- Adoption papers
- Military discharge papers/Veterans ID card

- Naturalization or Citizenship documents
- Power of Attorney for as long as it is valid
- Disability documentation
- Living Will/ Last Will and Testament
- documents relating to cemetery plots
- documents relating to beneficiaries
- Organ Donation Directives

Keep For Multiple years

- Deeds for property until sold
- Tax returns and documentation including business receipts for the past 7 years
- Passports are valid for ten years
- Mortgage contract and receipts until paid in full

- Title to a car until it is sold, transferred or discarded

- receipts for home improvements until all claims of major damage are settled

- Insurance policies and papers until the policy has expired or replaced

- Bank Statements should be kept for a year unless you have access to them online

- Receipts for any household appliance that is still under warranty

You need to keep files on all of the above documents labeled and in an order where you can easily find them.

Digital Clutter

If you hate your computer or don't even use one, you will need a file folder, properly labeled for any papers you want to keep. I love my computer and use it for so many different things. I retired from a job that required 90% of my work to be done on a computer so I have evolved as it has. It can become confusing and overwhelming at times.

You may find you have a collection of unwanted and unnecessary files that need to be cleaned out and sent to the digital trash bin. You have to find a schedule that works for you.

I have found if I do this clean-up of files once a month. That works pretty well for me, and now that I have most things organized already. It only takes a short amount of time to take care of all the new stuff. I don't have to search for hours trying to find what I need or want if they are all in the correct folder and properly labeled.

One indication that it's time to do some digital decluttering is when your downloads folder is a seemingly endless scroll of documents and images. Create folders categorized just like you would for paper file folders. Drag and drop or if you prefer, copy and paste each item into the folder that it should be in. This will make locating the files quick and easy. The rest of the files that are outdated or not needed should go directly to the digital trash bin and empty them.

Most other paperwork can be scanned and saved to a cloud file like google drive or

OneDrive or a folder in your computer. This would include any medical files and records. Vaccination records should also be kept. as well as records of surgeries and lists of all medications.

Go through your email and delete any items not helpful or needed then empty the associated trash and spam folders If you want, you can create folders in your email to make things easier to find. I have a folder there for email orders and receipts. If you go through your email daily it will take only minutes.

Take a good look at your desktop screen too. I sometimes have a lot of files I have put there until I have time to sort them into the proper folders. I found if I create a Miscellaneous or Stuff folder and put all my odds and ends there until I'm ready to deal with them keep my computer desktop neat and organized.

Photographs

Time and commitment are required once the decision has been made to organize your photos. It's not something you should procrastinate but you actually need to do. The longer I waited, the more it became confusing when sorting them. If you put it off you just continue collecting more photos and the job gets bigger and bigger. Now is the time to bite the bullet and get it done. Step one in the process is to collect all photos in one place. Locating all your photos is a challenge of its own. Start with any digital devices where they are currently stored such as PCs, tablets, and phones. Also, look for pictures on the internet or social media used by your family. Sort through your email for any photos you have sent or received.

Next, create a space for all your photo albums and boxed photos to be collected. Using a good-quality scanner, preserve your printed photo memories in high-resolution quality images. Removing duplicates or similar photos and cutting it down to the best two or three will help. Looking through them, I decided the best thing I could do was to sort out the bad ones that have faded beyond recognition and throw them away along with the blurred-out ones.

This was for me, one of the most challenging tasks I had to undertake. Scanning was not an issue even though it is quite time-consuming. The biggest hurdle I had to deal with was to decide how much storage would be required for the digital files and what form of categorization I wanted to set up. Sorting them into year folders works well for lots of pictures but I have many of my mother's and grandparents' pictures and don't have the exact year for those. These things apply to physical as well as digital files. I have hundreds or thousands of pictures of family, friends, and special occasions. Setting aside one day a week or month you can make slow but steady progress. I am still working on this project knowing that sometime in the future it can be passed on to my children and grandchildren in a very organized fashion.

I chose to go the digital route for my photos. Once I got through those steps, I decided to scan them all into the computer at a high resolution. The advantage of having digital copies is they will no longer fade, fold or tear. Perfect copies can be shared, printed on demand, and sorted into digital file folders.

Create a folder structure that is easy to remember and that you can use consistently for all your pictures in the future as well as now. You may choose to file by year and break down the years into subfolders for events or travel. Examples of subfolders would be "Family Christmas" or "Moms Birthday". For a travel vacation, the subfolders could be names of the different places visited during that vacation. Your folder "Ireland" with subfolders might be Dublin, Quiet Man Museum, and Trinity College. Others use a system separating family by family to include all the direct family members sort of like a family tree.

I would suggest you rename your digital photos. This is better done once your files are sorted into their correct folder and subfolders. Most digital sources will have strange names like DSCxxx or SCANxxx. An example would be to name them beginning with the year, month, day, and event. An example of this is 20160416-Pool Party. To rename all photos in the folder follow these steps:

Set the folder view to Details

1. Select all pictures by right click on the mouse and sorting by Date

2. right click your mouse on the first file and click Rename

3. Type in your selected information (for example 20160416-Pool Party) and Press Enter.

The files in this folder should now be renamed. Your system will automatically add a number in brackets at the end of the file name to represent the file sequence in the folder.

Some services can do the digitizing part for you and create disks or drives for storage This service can be quite expensive depending on the amount of items or videos you have. It was not an option for me. I took my time and did a stack at a time on weekends or watching TV at night. Once you have everything in order and organized you can create a backup of your files. To create your backup, go to your main folder named Photos or Pictures, right-click on the folder and select Copy. Go to your destination drive's main folder, right-click again, and select Paste. Now sit back and watch it work or take a break for a cup of coffee or tea. The amount of time this will take depends on the number of files it is copying and pasting over.

The frequency of backups should depend on how often you add photos or work on your pictures. Once this is done, I won't worry about losing any of those wonderful memories. This makes sharing them easy as they can be shared and sent to anyone I choose via email or shared folders in cloud storage. You should always make a backup of all the files and folders on some other platform such as an external drive but your backup copy should reside in a different location than your master files.

- **TIP:**

I know I just asked you to sit at a screen for a lengthy period of time. It should be part of your week to put down your phone, tablet, and computer for 24 hours. If that is too much to deal with, take small steps and put them down for an hour, and increase them bit by bit to a point where you are comfortable taking that time off. Try to stay aware of your posture while you use these devices as over time, bad posture can cause permanent damage to your spine. Putting down all the digital items might surprise you with the amount of free time you now have. Pain, eyestrain, blurred vision, and headaches can be caused by spending too much time in front of your screens. A pair of blue-blocking glasses can help with this. Even if it's required for your work, allow yourself to break once in a while by going to the printer or getting a cup of tea or coffee.

Attic, Basement, Garage

As you've worked on decluttering and organizing your home, you may have come across items that you couldn't decide whether to keep or let go. Instead of dealing with these items, you might have simply moved them to different areas, thinking it would make the rest of your home feel calm and orderly. This approach is only a short term solution that hides these items from view without truly addressing them.

You might think that you can skip dealing with these spaces altogether and of course that is your choice. Once you have finished organizing these areas it will add a sense of completion to what you have been working toward. Now it's a good idea to create an inventory list and display it on a wall near the back of the door. This way, you can easily maintain the area and quickly see what you have stored there. I'm sharing these ideas for those who are interested in organizing this way as well. Some of this is a bit repetitive but will help keep you on track when deciding on next steps.

Attics

We only sometimes think about the attic, especially when decluttering and organizing our home. Since I am happy with my progress in the rest of my home, I want to put this space to better use. Like other areas, it helps to have a goal and a good plan. That can make this much faster and easier than you thought. What is your desired result for your attic? Do you want it to continue being used for storage space, or do you want to turn it into a more useful space like an office or playroom? Part of that will depend on your needs and the space size.

To do the best job, I suggest removing everything from your attic. This gives you the best result and a better space to work in. Suppose that is not practical for you, Do your best to move everything to one side so you have room to sort things out. Most items in an attic are stored in boxes and bins. If you have something just sitting around, sort those things first. That gets them out of your way.

Like in other areas, have your labeled bags and boxes ready for the trash, donations, selling, or keeping. Finding items as you sort will turn up things you had completely forgotten. You may have some duplicate items. Some might be special for you, and some may not. Now's the time to decide what to keep and what you no longer need.

When you get everything out of your way, clean the space well. Use a vacuum to not just stir up the dust by sweeping. Lots of dust continuously collects in attics. As we advance, we occasionally repeat organizing and cleaning the space. Make a habit of checking on the area so your attic remains clutter-free.

Now that things are sorted assess the space and determine areas for storing related items together. By keeping like items together, you save time searching for something. Use storage bins to protect belongings, and they should be clear so you can see what is in them at a glance. Have a section for holiday items, and ensure bins have detailed labels so specific items are easily found when needed. On plastic containers, quickly attach a label, or you can write directly on the box with a permanent marker. Now when you put things away, it is easy to find the bin they go in. For example, Christmas ornaments, wreaths, or garlands. You might also have Easter, Forth of July, and other holiday décor to store in this section.

If you have seasonal pieces of furniture, they can have their own area. For items that don't fit in bins, add inexpensive shelving and cover the items with dust covers to save time cleaning them when you are ready to use them. Also, use dust covers for oversized items such as luggage. If the surfaces are not transparent, you can use a permanent marker to label them to identify them without looking under them to find things. Putting items used the most near the door is another way to save time.

Basement

If you have a basement, it may be a single large unused space or divided into separate, finished, or unfinished areas. Things accumulate there and can become a graveyard for unwanted or broken items you haven't found time to fix. You may have outdated electronics there that should have been removed long ago. (see the section on junk removal)

A few simple tips can help you take advantage of this space, so don't avoid this area. Instead, make a plan of action for this project, whether you want to do it all in a weekend or split it up into smaller parts to keep from being overwhelmed. It can be a dreadful task. This is especially true if you, like many others, have used this space to dispose of junk and unwanted items, keeping in mind you will get back to them in time to deal with them. Sometimes, out of sight means out of mind.

Get the trash out of the way first and get rid of it. To begin to declutter the basement, start with the most oversized items. Then, post anything you feel has value online or add to your yard sale items to make extra money. You can also recycle, upcycle or donate items to nonprofits, shelters, or thrift stores.

Garage

Your garage often becomes a space that is a catch-all for various items, from tools and sporting equipment to seasonal decorations and household supplies. However, an organized garage not only provides functional benefits but also enhances the overall appeal and efficiency of your home. Here, we will explore practical tips and strategies that will help transform your cluttered garage into a well-organized and functional space.

Using your outdoor equipment and tools or enjoying the space can be difficult if your garage is dirty and cluttered. Cleaning out the garage seems to be a job everybody hates, but if you plan and go step by step, you might be surprised how much you can get done on a sunny Saturday afternoon with good music in the background.

It is a big job, and it may take an entire weekend to get things the way you want. It's a big project, but it will reap considerable results. Once organized and cleaned, weekly or monthly maintenance should keep it in good shape year-round. There is no one-size-fits-all approach to organizing your garage, so tailor your plan to fit your family's lifestyle and schedule. After you plan for all the tasks to be completed, enlist other family members to complete this project. Assigning everyone jobs to be done will make the job go much quicker and easier.

Pull your vehicles out and get started. This includes items on hooks and any plastic totes. Before diving into the organization process, it's essential to declutter and sort through the items in your garage. Begin by emptying the entire space, creating a blank canvas to work with. As you go through each item, categorize them into groups such as tools, sports equipment, gardening supplies, automotive, and miscellaneous items. Take this opportunity to assess each item's usefulness and consider donating, selling, or discarding those you no longer need or haven't used in a long time. I know this is a bit repetitive but that will keep you focused and on track.

Trash accumulates here quickly, so clearing the trash and litter can make working in the space much easier. Tear down boxes and sweep or use a leaf blower to clear the floor. Knock down cobwebs and dust off the walls using a broom or extension duster. Now make decisions on any repairs that you would like to make or want. Scrub the floor with a mop or a push broom. Doing this in an empty space is just so much easier. Some might want to go as far as painting the walls and putting a new finish on the floor using epoxy or rubber flooring. These are time-consuming but some feel they are well worth the effort. It all depends on your schedule and your budget. Once that job is complete it's time to get started with the sorting and organizing.

Creating Zones To optimize your garage's functionality, consider dividing the space into distinct zones based on the different categories of items. For example, designate an area for tools, another for sporting equipment, and a separate section for gardening supplies. This zoning approach allows for easier navigation and ensures that items are stored logically and conveniently.

Investing in proper storage solutions is key to keeping your garage organized. Here are some ideas to consider:

1. Shelving and Cabinets: Install sturdy shelves or cabinets so that you can store frequently used items within easy reach. Label the shelves or use clear storage containers to help identify the contents quickly. You may find you have more storage space than you thought but keep the garage door and tract clear.

2. Pegboards and Wall Hooks: Utilize wall space by installing pegboards or hooks to hang tools, garden hoses, and other equipment. This saves floor space and keeps items visible and easily accessible.

3. Overhead Storage: Maximize vertical space by installing overhead storage racks or platforms. These are perfect for storing bulky items like seasonal decorations or rarely used equipment. You may find you have more storage space than you thought but keep the garage door and tract clear.

4. Clear Storage Containers: Store smaller items in transparent, stackable containers to keep them organized and easily visible. Label each container for quick identification.

5. Storage tubes are a great way to keep rakes, hoes, shovels and things upright and easily accessible. Keep gardening items together and brooms or other equipment in another. The tubes work well in the corners and eliminate a good amount of wasted space.

6. Plan for bicycles, camping gear, tools, and tool boxes.

A well-organized garage should also prioritize maintenance and safety. Consider the following tips:

1. Regular Cleaning: Dedicate time to clean your garage regularly, removing dust, cobwebs, and any potential hazards. This helps maintain a clean and pleasant environment.

2. Fire Safety: Ensure your garage is equipped with fire extinguishers and smoke detectors. Store flammable materials, such as gasoline and paint, in designated, secure cabinets away from ignition sources.

3. Tool Safety: Store sharp tools in a safe and secure manner, such as locking cabinets or wall-mounted racks. This keeps them away from children. Use proper safety measures when handling them.

This contributes to an overall sense of order and efficiency in your home. By decluttering, creating zones, implementing storage solutions, and maintaining safety, you can transform your garage into a well-organized space that accommodates your storage needs while making it easier to find and access items when you need them. With a some effort and planning, you can reclaim your garage and enjoy the benefits of an organized and functional space. Consider all the items that you can store above and on the walls. Keeping things up off the floor makes it much easier to maintain order and keep clean.

OUTDOOR SPACES- LAWN, PORCHES, PATIOS AND SHEDS

Your lawn, porches and Patios may be a project you undertake when spring cleaning or fall clean up and put away. That may be determined in part by the climate where you live.

This chapter will address the spaces you may not consider part of home organizing, but if you get them in order, you will enjoy sitting on the patio or swinging on the porch more with the clutter gone.

Many have seasonal decorations for their outdoor spaces. When changing out those for different seasons is a great time to sort through them and decide if some are worn or no longer enjoyed. Then decide whether to replace, donate, or dispose of them.

There may also be furnishings you have that are not appropriate for all seasons. Put them away to protect them from weathering to help declutter the area.

Seasonal items, including holiday or winter gear, can be stored in a shed, garage, or basement. If those are not options for you, get storage containers that you can store under benches, chairs or a patio table. Make sure they have labels so you can easily locate what you are looking for when you need it.

Porches

You may have a front porch, steps, or just a small doorway that is the entryway to your home. You want it to be neat and welcoming. Keep steps clear and ensure the front door has ample room to open completely.

Your porch might be where you like to hang out with family and friends or sit and read a book. Clear out the clutter for a nice walkway and enough space to open the door fully. Have enough seating or standing area for everyone to be comfortable who wants to join you. Small tables are useful for setting your drink or small snack.

Cleaning your outdoor furniture will lengthen the life of the pieces.

After the clutter is gone will be a good time to clean the floor and a good time to give it a new coat of paint or stain if needed. Now everything looks so nice that your porch was unused before may be used more often now when the weather is good.

Patios

A patio is a space the entire family can enjoy. If you have any broken or unused furniture, it is time to remove it. If it is in good condition, consider donating to a charitable organization. You can check with a seniors center to determine if they need it. Getting them out of the way makes cleaning easier and frees up more space.

If you want to replace some furniture, wicker or plastic can be a good choice that weathers well and requires little maintenance. When choosing chairs with cushions, ensure the fabric is durable and can withstand the elements. Perhaps, limit the number of accessories like potted plants, candles or statuettes. Too many of these can add to the cluttered look and feel of the space.

Keep your patio clean and inviting by sweeping or hosing down frequently. Make trash bins available and empty them often to keep the area more enjoyable, and you will be more likely to use the space. Remember that a dirty or cluttered patio is no fun for anyone.

If you love gardening, you can create a designated space for all your gardening supplies. Set up a shelf or a rolling cart for small items or if you are an avid gardener, invest in a gardening shed or even a small greenhouse.

Do you have an outdoor kitchen or even just an area with a grill? Put utensils or unused items away in a cabinet or on hooks to keep them together. Cleaning your grill after each use will make your next grilled meal much easier.

Having things clean and organized makes it more appealing and functional and creates a space you and your family will enjoy spending time outdoors and relaxing.

Sheds and Outdoor Storage

A shed is certainly unnecessary but a very nice thing to have. It can serve many purposes and keep other areas clutter-free. But what about the shed itself? Your shed can quickly become a catch-all.

Recognizing this fact makes it even more important to keep it void of clutter and organized. The best way to avoid this is not to put things there that you are just unprepared to deal with to get them out of your way. Make sure it has a purpose and uses the space to its best advantage.

Like all the other areas we have dealt with, the best attack is to remove everything from the shed and lay it out in the yard or driveway. Depending on the size of your shed and the number of items in it, it might take a day or even an entire weekend. Not a job you want to undertake on a rainy day.

Now that everything is out in the open take the opportunity to sort out all the clutter of broken items never repaired, duplicates bought because you couldn't find the one you had, and any other items you no longer want or need.

When sorting, consider the effect moisture, temperature, and pests can have. Some items may be better stored in another place because of this. Go through each thing and evaluate slowly for each type of item.

Trash and broken items you know you will never repair should be disposed of, and any duplicate or unwanted items in good condition can be donated. The senior citizen center near me has an area for gardening. They might be happy to have some extra gardening tools on hand.

Before putting anything back in the shed, clean it out and eliminate any webs or bugs. Now would be a good time to spray around the interior and exterior walls to keep out those little pests.

Now that re-homed items are out of the way and the trash is gone, it is time to think about how you want to organize your shed. Take some time and sort through the remainder. Keeping items in groups such as gardening tools, propane, or fuel cans or tanks. When sorted, you can create an organized plan for the space.

Cardboard boxes are great for organizing but not in a shed. before you put all those shovels and ladders back in, consider what kind of storage you need. Adjust what you have done in the past and think about the best options in the future.

Check any storage bins that are cracked and no longer useful, and remove any bent shelves. If budget allows, invest in leakproof bins of appropriate sizes and shelving for items better stored on shelves.

Small garden tools can be stored on hooks, and installing a magnetic strip is a good idea for things like screwdrivers, pliers, and wrenches to keep them out of the way. Cleaning all tools before placing them back in the shed provides longer life to the tools and helps keep the shed clean.

Before just tossing items in the shed, consider how they will affect future use of the shed and how it might block access to other items.

When you add new items to the shed, be sure you are deliberate about their placement. If you return anything you take out and use to its assigned storage place, your shed will stay organized and useful in the future.

Organize your Car

Forgetting something you need reminds you that when you are out and about, consider your car an extension of your home. This can be especially true if you have children. Keeping essentials on hand makes your trip much easier and nearly stress-free. Having your home in order, this might be one more place you would like to have some organization.

It can be a safety factor to be able to find the items you need during an emergency. Those include a flashlight and a small tool to break out a window if you have an accident and a fire or your vehicle lands in the water. These should be within easy reach. Also, consider having a sharp knife if the seat belts won't open.

Of course, before organizing, it is essential to clean and take out all the trash. You can find a small hand-held vacuum that easily fits under the seat or in the trunk. This makes it quick and easy to keep up with crumbs, leaves, and dirt to keep clean up on the go. If you procrastinate cleaning your windshield wipers or replacing them if necessary, remember they can dry out and crack quickly. To prolong their life, soak a rag in window cleaner and wipe them down from one end to the other as you clean the windshield.

When you get to the glove box, to keep it neat and paperwork accessible when needed, a small plastic file folder keeps everything in order, like those used to organize coupons when shopping. Small headrest hooks can keep a purse or bag out of the way and not fly off the seat when you stop. If you have a car full of tablets or phones, be sure you have a place for everyone to plug in and recharge when needed.

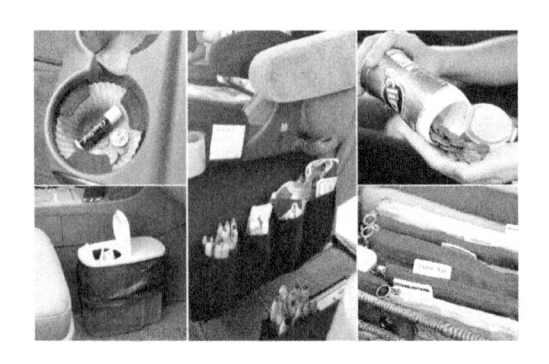

An easy DIY air freshener can be made using scented candle wax in a small jar with a metal or plastic lid. Just put in the wax and put some holes in the top. It easily fits under the seat and is completely out of the way. Is that not an option you like? Buy an essential oil dispenser and clip it on the vent. Use a soothing scent such as lavender that gives a bit of calm in a chaotic kid-filled car. Other options are a clip-on air freshener on the visor or one that hangs from the rearview mirror.

Last but not least, your car has a trunk. Some things to ensure you have with you are jumper cables, a spare tire, and a jack. Having a first aid kit is great, and I always keep a roll of paper towels and cleaning wipes. A tire pressure gauge and learn how to use it. What happens if you get a flat in the rain?

Have a couple of inexpensive rain ponchos to keep dry if you must step out of the car to deal with a problem. If you prefer, you can keep an umbrella. A battery-powered light to mark where your car is pulled over makes you and your family much safer.

You can find many more tools and gadgets if you shop around. With these things to rely on, you will have greater peace of mind and feel safer when traveling alone or with your family.

Options for Junk Removal

The least expensive option is to haul things away to their proper places, but there are other options.

If it is within your budget, you can hire a junk removal company to come to your home and pick up items you no longer want or need. That might save you a trip to the dump.

The fees for this service will depend on the quantity, weight, and size of your items to be picked up and also the part of the country you live in. Heavier pieces will raise the cost a bit too.

I would get an estimate from three services and also check their reviews. If they have a lot of negative reviews, you should work with one that is more reputable.

Ask these questions before hiring. How will you haul the junk away? What kind of space will the vehicle you bring need? Are there things you will not haul away, such as old tires, open paint cans, asbestos, or toxic things like oil drums and solvents?

Clear a path and move other vehicles out of the way or have everything in one place. Let them know you will have a heavy piano or furniture. Ask if they want everything outside or can carry the items out of your home. This will be important to know In choosing what company you will use.

Most junk removal services will pick up the following:

- Trash

- Carpeting

- Mattresses

- Yard Waste

- furniture

- appliances

- Electrical equipment(see options below for electronics)

- Renovation Debris

- Scrap metal

Some services will even tear down that old shed or barn and haul it away. Make sure to distinguish this type of service from a dumpster rental. Junk removal will bring their own containers to fill with your items and haul them away. The dumpster rental will drop the dumpster at your location and return later to pick it up. You can tell them how long you need it or when they should schedule the pickup.

You will find some services that provide both. Being at home during pickup is beneficial to ensure they get everything and answer any questions or concerns. Find out what payment method they accept. If you choose them, leave a review of their service, or you can even agree to be a future reference.

Sometimes, you may find a free junk removal that will pick up your things to recycle or redistribute items, and there is their payment. For example, charitable organizations like Salvation Army and Goodwill will pick up for free if you have many bags of clothing and household goods. They may offer to pick up furniture as well. Call them to find out if this service is available and to schedule the pickup.

Another free option is to set things by the side of the road in front of your home with a sign to indicate the items are free to take.

If recycling is important to you, find a removal service that has a dedicated space and staff to sort items and properly recycle all of their collected items. Ask them the question before you hire them to find out if this is part of their service. For example, 80 to 90 percent of mattress materials can be recycled.

Contact your local recycling center for info on things that cannot be recycled in your area. Curbside recycling systems have directories on what types of plastics can be added to your bin, some even with pictures and materials definitions. One of the newest tools, created by The Recycling Partnership, allows you to chat with a virtual assistant that tells you what you can recycle."

"Can You Recycle Recycled Items?

It depends on the material. Plastics can only be recycled once or twice before turning into something else, like clothing. Paper may be recycled about eight times before it's turned into a paste destined for egg cartons or newspaper. But glass and metal? They can be recycled repeatedly — infinitely — making them the ultimate eco-friendly materials." John Shegerian - Recycle Nation 2017

For large amounts of yard waste, call your trash removal company. They may offer to pick up your yard debris or even your Christmas tree and dispose of it for free if properly bagged.

Working electronics can be donated or sold on eBay, Facebook Marketplace, or Craigslist. Broken items should be sent to a recycling center, retailer, or manufacturer. (see paragraph below for details) Many old electronics contain heavy metals and some hazardous materials. Freon can be collected from air conditioners and refrigerators before the remainder is recycled. Some things that can't be recycled are specific batteries, light bulbs, plastic, and glass. Other things that are not recyclable are sewing needles, garden hoses, and propane tanks or cylinders.

What should you do to prepare items to be donated or traded in? First, learn How to Wipe Your Cellphone Clean. The process is the same whether you have a basic phone or a smartphone. Locate the settings menu and look for the factory reset option. You should find it easy on a basic phone. For smartphones, you might have to click through a few different menus.

- **iPhones:** Settings > General > Reset > Erase all Content and Settings

- **Android phones:** Settings > System > Reset (or Backup & Reset) > Factory Data Reset > Reset Phone > Erase Everything

Back up everything you want to save to a cloud service or your phone's backup program. After you delete personal data, remove the SIM card, and deactivate your phone from your service provider's network. Now you are ready to donate or recycle your phone.

Local centers, schools, libraries, adult education, and employment programs may accept your used electronics and related accessories. Homeless shelters and domestic violence centers. Senior centers or assisted living facilities will sometimes be looking for cell phones, computers, and TVs. Call before you drop off any working electronics to find out what they need or will accept. Your old electronics can be donated if they are:

- less than five years old

- function reliably

- Major repairs or replacement of parts is not required.

There are options to keep in mind regarding electronics that can depend on what kind of items you are dealing with. If you have old smartphones or tablets and are planning to upgrade your device, contact the manufacturer or retailer. Amazon has a program for mailing in your Bluetooth speakers, phones, tablet, or e-readers and will send you a gift card. If you have an Apple device, they offer credits on new computers, iPad, iPhones, and Apple watches if you trade in your older item. BestBuy has a recycling program, but you should call ahead to check that the location near you accepts the items. They have a trade-in estimator specifically for cell phones. Call2Recycle also has a recycling program and often places drop boxes at retailers such as Lowe's, Home Depot, and UbreakIfix for rechargeable batteries and cell phones. HP also offers return and recycle options for old computers.

Check with your city to find out if they have events to assist residents in responsibly getting rid of old electronics. Find out if they have this sort of event near you by calling your city's service department. Ask where to drop items off and what kind of products are accepted.

"A ... misconception is that the products a homeowner could recycle are not valuable, so not recycling is not that big of a deal. These materials, especially plastic products, are extremely valuable and have the potential to be recycled and reused. There is value in the collection of plastic materials because the demand for recycled content is snowballing. And as technology advances and innovations evolve, recycled content can now be processed back into food packaging, medical products, and industrial applications. Additionally, using recycled content reduces the need for natural resources during the production of virgin resin." **Andy Brewer, Associate Director of Sustainability & Materials, Plastics Industry Association**

Plan for Maintaining Order

Now that you have gone through your home, getting rid of clutter, and organizing the things you've chosen to keep, it's time to plan to keep up the excellent work. You probably have done much of this for each room as you have completed it. If so, great job. If you want some tips on keeping it organized, we will give you some in this chapter. Now we can work through a typical day and find out how.

Remember the Marine's "Make and Wake". Completing this in the morning leaves you with a feeling of achievement that will continue throughout your day and inspire you to do more. Once this becomes a habit, it will no longer feel like a chore.

Mornings are a great time to empty the dishwasher while you enjoy your tea or coffee. If time allows, you can start a load of laundry before heading out to work. If you don't work outside the home, like a stay-at-home Mom or retiree, sit down to enjoy reading, watching the news, taking a walk, or enjoying your hobby.

Small things done as you go are an excellent way to maintain order. If something takes less than a minute, do it. For example, please don't put that coffee or tea cup in the sink. Instead, take that extra few seconds to put it in the dishwasher. As you pass through a room on your way to another, look around and pick up anything you can deposit in its proper place as you go by. When you bring in the mail, discard all the junk mail immediately and put bills or items that need attention in a designated place. While you heat something in the microwave, look around and see what can be done during the set time. If you spend 20 to

30 minutes daily, you will have much less to do on weekends. Tackling one room a day goes a long way.

Make a quick sweep nightly with a basket to pick up everything out of place. This keeps rooms tidy. The items can be put away at a later time if you like. For example, quickly wipe down the bathroom at night during your getting ready for bed routine. Next, put away the things left out during the day. If done nightly, it will only take a couple of minutes.

Stopping clutter at the door helps contain the chaos. Jackets, pocket items, shoes, and bags should all have a drop zone by the door. Have a designated place for keys, sunglasses, phones, and small items to be kept until heading out the door again. A small basket or bowl might be enough but have a space for every family member to make it easy. Set up a place for phones to be recharged when not in use.

Once a week, take time to scan in and save your documents. File things like insurance documents, invoices, and invitations. Set notifications on your computer, phone, or to-do list. for a reminder of due dates or special occasions, saving money on late fees, and avoiding missing essential events. Suppose you clean out your refrigerator every week. In that case, you will no longer have to deal with those nasty "science projects" (moldy leftovers) that accumulate there. If you do this the day before your trash pickup, then done and gone.

Create a schedule or plan to go through storage areas, perhaps once a month, so things don't accumulate. Check for expired food in the pantry. Check the kitchen drawers for duplicate items or things you no longer use. Be sure to revisit those junk drawers, too, so junk doesn't just get tucked in to get it out of sight. If you don't need it, let it go.

Keep all household members involved by assigning chores and understanding responsibilities to maintain your organization. The back of the book includes a chart you can print to keep up with the task each one is responsible for. When everyone does their chores for a week without nagging or whining, Give everyone a treat or an allowance. If it's just you, have yourself that favorite chocolate, bowl of ice cream, or glass of wine.

Below is a list of 50 tasks that take 5 to 10 minutes to complete that help maintain order and organization in your home. Do these frequently and soon they will become habits that you do without a second thought. I'm sure you will find many more to add to the list.

1. Sweep one floor

2. Mop one floor

3. Wipe out the microwave

4. Clean out the kitchen sink

5. Wipe down two countertops

6. Unload the dishwasher

7. Organize silverware drawer

8. Wipe off the stove

9. Clean toaster or toaster oven

10. set oven to self-clean

11. De-clutter the fridge

12. organize one Pantry shelf

13. Reorganize one kitchen cupboard

14. Clean out one drawer

15. Dust one ceiling fan

16. Wipe off the washer and dryer

17. Clean out your purse

18. Sort the mail

19. Throw in a load of laundry

20. water plants

21. Clean your computer screen

22. Answer 5 emails or texts

23. Clean bathroom mirrors

24. Dust a bookcase

25. Clean the bathroom sink

26. Clean computer or cell phone screen

27. Dust living room tables

Conclusion

In conclusion, This No-nonsense Guide to Organizing Your Home is a comprehensive guide to transforming your living space into a serene and functional haven. Throughout this book, we have explored a variety of strategies and techniques that can be applied to every room, helping you tackle clutter, maximize storage, and cultivate a sense of calm within your home.

How do you feel about all the extra space you discovered? How nice is knowing exactly where things are when you need them instead of spending endless hours looking for your keys, bag, hat, or gloves? Finding the exact pair of shoes, you want when you get dressed is excellent.

Organizing your home may seem overwhelming initially. Still, it can be a fulfilling and rewarding experience with the right mindset and tools.

Not only does an organized home lead to a more efficient and productive lifestyle, but it can also bring inner peace and harmony to your daily routine.

Remember to start small and tackle one room at a time, letting go of unnecessary possessions and implementing storage solutions that work for you. Stay focused, set achievable goals, and keep a positive attitude throughout the process.

Whether you are a busy professional, parent, or retiree, organizing your home can provide numerous benefits and set you toward a more balanced and serene life.

I hope that you have found the information contained here has helped you in some way to relieve stress, save time, money and find your motivation. These are only some of the advantages of having a more organized home. My journey has given me more time to do the things I love and some extra money to use for vacation, the house, or to spend on my grand-kids.

With the clutter gone, I am much calmer and enjoy life more without all the distractions. By recognizing the physical and psychological benefits of an organized living environment, we have laid the foundation for a holistic approach to organizing. From understanding the principles of mindful consumption to implementing practical storage solutions and establishing efficient routines, we have provided the tools necessary to navigate the challenges of organizing your home.

Moreover, we have emphasized the importance of personalized systems that suit your lifestyle and preferences. By recognizing that organizing is not a one-size-fits-all endeavor, we have encouraged you to adapt and modify the techniques presented to fit your unique needs. Whether you reside in a small apartment or a spacious house or live alone or with a family, this book has offered practical advice applicable to any situation.

Once you feel how well organized you are, keep up the good work, and if you just put things in their place after each use and pick up as you go, you will easily maintain that sense of well-being. Home has become a place I like to be. I hope you found this to be true for you as well.

In addition to the physical aspects of organization, we have explored the emotional and mental aspects as well. By addressing the psychological attachments to our belongings and the emotions tied to clutter, we have empowered you to overcome obstacles and develop a mindset that supports an organized and harmonious living space.

As you embark on your journey to organize your home, remember that it is not a destination but a continuous process. With persistence and dedication, you can create a home that reflects your values, fosters tranquility, and supports your overall well-being.

By incorporating the principles and strategies this book outlines, you can transform your home into a space that genuinely nurtures and inspires you.

Just a reminder that a QR code and link with instructions to some free worksheets are at the end of the book for your use. Feel free to make and print or use a digital copy and use them to help you achieve and maintain your wonderfully organized sanctuary.

So, take the first step today. Embrace the power of organization and embark on a path toward a more simplified, decluttered, and harmonious home. Your future self will thank you for the time and effort invested in creating a living environment that brings you joy, peace, and balance and learn to love your home again.

"It does not matter how slowly you go so long as you do not stop."
-Confucius

We can all learn to live with less clutter and be happier!

BONUS CHAPTER: CLEANING SOLUTIONS

Going through your home and getting things in order has been rewarding. Here are some cleaning tips to help along the way and beyond. Cleaning does not always have to be chemical-laden to be effective. Some of them are natural and inexpensive as well as effective.

They can only solve some cleaning problems, but I found them helpful. Some of these can save you time and money too.

Here are some cleaning staples to keep on hand and their benefits.

- Vinegar is super cheap, and it is a natural disinfectant. Use either apple cider vinegar or white distilled vinegar. Apple cider smells a little better, but be sure and dilute it with water before use.

- Baking Soda is an excellent deodorizer often used as a gentle scrub. It is inexpensive and natural.

- Hydrogen peroxide is a powerful oxidizer and is great for removing stains.

The Centers for Disease Control(CDC) states it kills bacteria, viruses, yeasts, mold spores, and fungi.

- Lemon peel has anti-fungal and antimicrobial properties. It also smells clean, and the oil can moisturize wood surfaces.

- Borax, Dawn, Fels Naphtha, Murphy's Oil Soap, Bar Keepers Friend, and WD-40

Having the right tool for the job is essential and makes it easy to keep your surfaces clean. Here is a list of some of those tools.

- reusable rags, paper towels, old newspapers, or coffee filters

- bucket or bowl

- lidded glass jar

- rubber gloves

- old T-shirts or socks

- sponges and brushes

- microfiber cloth

Now you are ready for those cleaning list jobs. Let's get started with the vinegar.

Vinegar

1. Bacteria live on your computer keyboard. An easy solution uses an old toothbrush dipped in equal parts vinegar and water. Scrub on and between the keys to eliminate germs.

2. Mixed 2 parts vinegar and 1 part water used in a spray bottle to clean all the glass surfaces in your home. They will sparkle and shine for a streak-free surface polish with old newspaper or coffee filters.

3. Use it to disinfect your countertops and kill germs eliminating that bleach smell permeating the area. If you have a tough stain, drop a small amount of dish

soap in to give it a boost. Please DO NOT use it on porous surfaces like granite.

4. The next item is the coffee pot. Equal parts vinegar and water. Run a cycle to eliminate buildup here. This works for a Keurig or any coffee machine to remove any buildup.

5. Water stains on your glasses can be removed using equal parts vinegar and water. Let it sit for 15 minutes. Scrub the stains away using a brush or a non-scratch pad, rinse, and wipe clean.

6. To remove calcium deposits on faucets and shower heads, mix 2 teaspoons of vinegar with 1 teaspoon of salt and wipe them down. If some buildup is still there, spray them directly with vinegar and tie a plastic bag around them to sit overnight. Scrub and rinse the following day, and that should do the trick. Use a dryer sheet to polish the fixtures to make them shine.

7. You thought harsh chemical cleaners would be the only way to deal with showers, tubs, toilets, and sinks. Spray on the vinegar and let it set for a few minutes. You might have to scrub, but it's better than having toxic fumes from other cleaners. Add a little baking soda and vinegar for the toilet, let it set to loosen up stains, and rinse. The bowl should be clean and deodorized.

8. If your microwave smells stinky, put ¼ cup vinegar and 1 cup water in a bowl, heat for a few minutes. This will loosen up any foodstuff and deodorize it. Wipe the dirt out with a cloth or paper towel.

9. Make your own fabric deodorizer by mixing equal parts of water, vinegar, and your favorite essential oil. Spray it on the upholstery to eliminate odors hanging out there.

10. Clean silver that has tarnished at home just by using vinegar. Mix 1 tbsp water,

and 1 tbsp vinegar, with 2-3 drops of dish soap. Let the jewelry soak in this mixture for around 15-30 minutes. Use a soft bristle brush, gently scrub off dirt or grime and rinse the jewelry. Wipe it off with a soft cloth. It is safe to use on your best diamond rings and won't damage them.

11. To dry clean your carpets, sprinkle with baking soda and sprinkle or spray with vinegar. Let stand for about an hour and then vacuum. The room will smell fresher too.

12. Cover heavy grease stains with a paste of baking soda. Spray with vinegar and let it sit for about 10 minutes to remove the stains in the pans.

13. When cleaning tiles, wet a cloth with vinegar or spray it on the tiles and rub it down to remove most dirt and it doesn't leave a film. It also works to remove scum from the shower doors.

14. Vinegar is ideal as a laundry detergent as it is tough on stains and odors. Put 1 cup of distilled white vinegar into the wash and let it run! Who Knew?

15. If you want to clean all the grime and dirt buildup from your window tracks, you only need baking soda and white vinegar. Use an old toothbrush to pull it out and make your window tracks shine again.

Baking Soda

1. Get stinky out of your refrigerator. Sprinkling baking soda around in your fridge won't scrub away any dried food or grime, but putting a small open box or cup in your fridge can help keep it smelling fresh. If mixed into a paste with vinegar and a drop of dish soap, it can help with stains and scum.

2. Eliminate stains and dirt with baking soda because it is a soluble salt. It can

also soften water, and then you need less detergent. Add ½ cup of baking soda to laundry detergent for cleaner clothes when doing laundry.

3. Boil 8-10 cups of water and add a cup of baking soda to it. Put the dirty stove filter in this mixture and continue boiling for 5-10 minutes.

4. Another option for cleaning the toilet is using baking soda and hydrogen peroxide. Evenly distribute half a cup of baking soda throughout the entire toilet bowl, and then proceed to pour hydrogen peroxide on top of it. Let it stand for 10-15 minutes to let the hydrogen peroxide and baking soda mixture work on it. Then scrub with your toilet brush. Flush and all the scum and dirt are gone.

5. A baking soda paste on a sponge is excellent for ovens, stained marble, grease, and tarnished silver. I also use it to clean my brass candlesticks. Wipe

them down with a wet rag until the residue is gone.

6. This works on carpet stains. Dust baking soda on the stain and spray it with water and vinegar. Give the area time to dry, and then use a brush to loosen the powder. Now you can vacuum up the remainder.

7. According to a study on apples, soak your produce in a baking soda wash. That is the best way to remove pesticides without peeling.

8. If you've burned something in one of your pots or pans, try boiling a mix of water and baking soda empty, use a scouring pad, and then rinse.

9. Baking soda has a high sodium content and can destroy weeds. Sprinkle it over the weeded area and watch them wither away. Please DO NOT use it in flower beds because it can kill plants other than weeds.

Lemons

1. Easy all-purpose cleaner: Fill a jar with a lid with lemon peels and white vinegar. Please put it in the pantry and let set for a few weeks. Mix the solution with equal parts of water. You just turned a science project into a cleaner!

2. If you have a garbage disposal that needs detoxing, run water and add pieces of lime or lemon down the drain to freshen it.

3. Microwaves: Take ½ cup of water and squeeze half a lemon into a microwave-safe container. Put the peel of the lemon in the water and nuke the mixture for two or three minutes until

steam coats the microwave. Now wipe it out with a clean rag, sponge, or paper towel. All clean!

4. Cutting Boards: To deodorize and clean off the food, take half a lemon and work it into the cutting board to clean off the food. If it has stains, sprinkle it with baking soda too. Wipe it off with clean water and dry it off.

5. Using a kettle for hot water could have mineral buildup after a while. Boil the kettle of water with some lemon peel. Let sit for about an hour and rinse. Nice and clean, and ready to make that next soothing cup of tea.

6. Polishing Wood. (Not to be used on hardwood floors-makes them slippery!) Mix ½ cup of lemon and 1 cup of vinegar added to 1 cup of olive oil. Rub the mixture on the wood with a soft cloth or rag, and the wood will shine like new. It doesn't store well, so mix it up when you

have time to polish all those wooden surfaces.

Hydrogen Peroxide(3%)

1. You love your cat but not that stinky litter box. To help minimize the smell, wash the box as usual and spray it with peroxide. Let it sit, rinse, and dry before filling it with new litter.

2. Many make-up brushes are made from animal hair. What do you wash your hair with? Shampoo, of course. Soak the bristles in a bowl of water with a teaspoon of 3% hydrogen peroxide for 10 minutes. Rinse them and let them air dry.

3. According to a recent study, 83% of dishwashers have fungi, and 47% tested positive for black yeast. Add ¼ cup of peroxide to the dishwasher with or without dishes and run the cycle to clean it up.

4. Accumulation of soap scum can be cleaned up by making a paste of ¼ cup vinegar, adding 1 cup baking soda plus 2 tablespoons of peroxide. When the bubbles form, scrub the surface and rinse. Suitable for sinks, showers, and tubs.

5. Another tip on your cutting board, USDA research states undiluted peroxide can destroy E.coli and Salmonella bacteria on cutting boards and counters. Apply it and let it set for 10 minutes. You can also soak wood cutting boards in peroxide for the same length of time.

6. After you clean your sink with baking soda, rinse with peroxide, let it set, and then rinse to kill germs.

Miscellaneous Quick Cleaning Hacks

1. Add 4 – 5 tablespoons of Borax to the wash for cleaner laundry.

2. Using 3 ingredients, you can easily make your glass stovetop look like new. You will need dish soap, baking soda, and hydrogen peroxide. First, apply dawn soap, then baking soda, and in the end, hydrogen peroxide over the stovetop. Some scrubbing might be required using your fingers or a soft brush to mix and spread evenly. Leave it for 3 or 4 minutes and wipe clean with a soft cloth. Voila! The stovetop is clean.

3. Denture tablets are one way to get the gunk out of your coffeepot. Put a couple of tablets where the water goes and run a couple of cycles to get rid of the gunk.

4. Use Borax to get rid of those hard water rust stains. Pour it on a damp rag and scrub the stain. Rinse and done. Borax is also a disinfectant. It inhibits many organisms, including bacteria, mold, and fungi.

5. Here is a surprising cleaning aid. Use

WD-40 to remove spilled glue, even super glue, off of fingers. It can also take hair dye stains out of towels.

6. WD-40 will remove crayons and markers from the walls.

7. Spray the front grill of your car with WD-40 to keep bugs from sticking or make them easier to clean off after driving.

8. WD-40 might also take scuff marks off your floor if mopping doesn't.

9. After removing labels from jars, WD-40 will take off the sticky residue.

10. When your child gets gum in their hair, use WD-40 to get it out instead of peanut butter.

11. Ketchup works wonders to clean your copper pans, and it's inexpensive and natural.

12. After the barbeque: You can clean up

that grill using an onion cut in half. Scrubbing it with the onion gets it done without any wire bristles left behind.

13. Add warm water, baking soda, and soap to clean your blender easily. Blend it for a few seconds. When done, rinse with clean water, or if you want, put it in the dishwasher to have it squeaky clean for the next use.

14. Clean and sanitize sponges by damping them and heating them in the microwave for 2 minutes. Now wipe out the microwave to remove any debris.

15. A washcloth or rag with several drops of lavender or orange essential oil can replace dryer sheets in the dryer with your clean laundry.

16. Tackle the grime stuck to your cookie sheets and pans using dryer sheets. Add soap, warm water, and a dryer sheet to warm water in your sink. Soak the pan for an hour or two. The mess washes

down the drain when you rinse.

17. Spraying or pouring vodka, then dab away odor and stains from pet accidents and red wine. It may smell boozy for a short time.

18. Another use for vodka is to get rid of mildew in the bathroom. Add a 50-50 mix of vodka and water in a spray bottle, spray the mildew area, and let set for about 10 minutes. Wipe with a clean cloth, and you are done. The alcohol in the vodka cleans the mess and kills the mildew.

19. Use a pillowcase to clean dust from individual ceiling fan blades. Wipe both sides using both hands. When done, just put the pillowcase in the wash. You can use an old sock if that works better for you.

20. If your fur baby leaves pet hair all over your furniture, put on a rubber glove and pet it, giving it a good rub-down.

Take the rubber glove off outside and wash it off so you don't clog up your sink.

21. Reuse the newspaper if you subscribe. The papers work great on glass instead of paper towels. Putting them in damp shoes will help soak up the moisture and the odors.

22. If you have silver and no silver cleaner, you can still get tarnished pieces shining again using toothpaste. Apply the toothpaste to the item and rub it with a cloth or rag. If the article has any ornate designs, you can use a toothbrush. Wipe off the residue when done.

23. Faucets and handles can shine again by rubbing them down with wax paper. The wax leaves a coating that will repel water and prevent future stains.

24. Or electronics(TVs, Monitors, etc.), you can use coffee filters as screen dusters. They don't scratch those surfaces or

leave fibers behind.

25. If you own cast iron pans or skillets, use olive oil and salt with a stiff brush. It cleans cooked-on gunk. You can also use a potato cut in half with salt to scrub with.

26. For difficult stains on your upholstery, rub shaving cream (not gel) into the stain and let set for 30 minutes or more, then blot dry. Test it on an unnoticeable spot to be sure it doesn't affect the fabric's color.

27. If you want to make your own dish soap, use castile soap(made from plant oil). A small amount goes a long way, using 1 part castile soap to 10 parts water. Works great.

ADDITIONAL STATISTICS

35 additional statistics related to Clutter and Organization

List by https://www.organizedinteriors.com/blog/home-organization-statistics/

1. It's estimated that only 20% of the things we own are actually used. (LexisNexis study)

2. 97% of surveyed realtors believe homeowners covet closet space more than a basement and attic storage space. (Braun Research survey)

3. It's estimated we'll spend 3,680 hours searching for misplaced items in our lifetime. (The Daily Mail)

4. 1 in 9 women were late for work because they could not find some part of their outfit to wear. (OnePoll survey)

5. Disorganization results in 23% of adults paying their bills late and incurring late payment fees. (Harris Interactive study)

6. Mortgage data research firm HSH.com ranked homeowners' pet peeves, with lack of storage space coming in first at 67%.

7. 10% of women say they feel depressed every time they open their closet doors. (OnePoll survey of 1,000 American women)

8. 63% of those surveyed planned to get rid of outdated clothing in the next year. (MSN.com poll)

9. removing clutter would eliminate approximately 40% of the housework in the average home. (Soap and Detergent Association study)

10. 57% of women believe that a closet that's organized makes it easier and quicker to find what they need. (OnePoll survey)

11. A study of 2,137 U.S. women revealed that their closets had an average of $550 worth of unworn clothing. (10 Yetis survey)

12. Even with the popularity of smartphones and with many home organization apps available, only 8% of survey respondents regularly used an app to help with home organization. (Moen survey)

13. Women with shoe racks are 7 times more likely to be on time for work than those without. (IKEA study)

14. 47% of women struggle when it comes to deciding on which work outfit they should wear. (OnePoll survey)

15. A new child in a household increases the inventory of possessions by 30% during the preschool years alone for a family. (UCLA study)

16. 1 in 6 women have resorted to taking dirty clothes out of their laundry hamper when they're unable to find anything to wear. (One Poll survey)

17. 40% of Australians say they feel guilty, depressed, or anxious about their home clutter. (Australia Institute study)

18. 50% of American women do some type of housework each day, compared to 22% of men. (Bureau of Labor Statistics study)

19. 61% of women who have difficulty finding anything in their closets buy new clothes. (OnePoll survey)

20. Disorganization (not lack of space) causes 80% of household clutter. (Soap and Detergent Association study)

21. The average U.S. home has 4 closets. (OnePoll survey)

22. The garage, kitchen, and home office were named the most cluttered spaces in homes. (Moen survey)

23. It's estimated that 80% of your clothes are only worn 20% of the time. (National Association of Professional Organizers study)

24. In a survey of 1,000 American women, 1 in 4 described their closets as being disorganized. (OnePoll survey)

25. 67% of people surveyed believe they could save up to 30 minutes a day if they were more organized. (Alpha Phi Quarterly study)

26. Phones, keys, sunglasses, and paperwork are the most commonly misplaced items in homes. (The Daily Mail)

27. Americans waste more than nine million hours daily looking for lost and misplaced items. (Ottawa Citizen)

28. 44% of women polled say they're unable to find an item in their closet at least once a month. (OnePoll survey)

29. An international retailer's survey found that 31% of its customers were more satisfied after closing their closets than after sex. (New York Times)

30. Worrying about their home isn't clean or organized enough is Americans' 5th most com-

mon stress trigger. 47% say this caused stress within the past month. (Huffington Post survey)

31. The closet of the average American woman contains 103 items. (OnePoll survey)

32. 80% of our medical expenses are related to stress, which clutter contributes to. (The Centers for Disease Control and Prevention study)

33. The average U.S. home has approximately 300,000 things. (L.A. Times)

34. 3 in 10 women say an organized closet would make their mornings less stressful. (OnePoll survey)

35. The Daily Mail reports that the average value of the contents in Britons' homes has increased 133% in the past 30 years.

FREE PLANNER ACCESS LINK AND QR CODE

URL and QR code to the free Planner/Workbook.

bit.ly/44HpZkq

SCAN ME

ACKNOWLEDGEMENTS

1. Kondo, M. (n.d.). The Life-Changing Magic of Tidying Up: The Japanese Art of Decluttering and Organizing (Vol. 1). Ten Speed Press. Retrieved April 25, 2023, from https://www.amazon.com/Life-Changing-Magic-Tidying-Decluttering-Organizing/dp/1607747308

2. "7 Mind-Blowing Home Organization Statistics to Help You Get Organized." ABC Closets. Retrieved from https://www.abclosets.com/7-mind-blowing-home-organization-statistics-to-help-you-get-organized/

3. Brewer, A. (2018). 'Andy Brewer, Associate Director of Sustainability & Materials, Plastics Industry Association'. Budget Dumpster. Available at: https://www.budgetdumpster.com/blog/andy-brewer-associate-director-of-sustainability-materials-plastics-industry-association/ (Accessed: May 8, 1923).

4. Shegerian, J. (n.d.). "How Many Times Can Recyclables Be Recycled?" Recycle Nation. Retrieved from https://recyclenation.com/2017/06/how-many-times-can-recyclables-be-recycled/ (Accessed: May 8, 2023).

5. Caputo, L., et al. (2018). "Antimicrobial and antibiofilm activities of citrus water-extracts obtained by microwave-assisted and conventional methods." PubMed Central. Retrieved from https://www.ncbi.nlm.nih.gov/pmc/articles/PMC6026940/

6. "Chemical disinfectants." (2008). Centers for Disease Control and Prevention. Retrieved from https://www.cdc.gov/infectioncontrol/guidelines/disinfection/disinfection-methods/chemical.html

7. "Cleaning and sanitizing the kitchen." (2010). Colorado State University Extension. Retrieved from https://extension.colostate.edu/docs/pubs/foodnut/kitchen-sanitize.pdf

8. De Castillo, M. C., et al. (2000). "Bactericidal activity of lemon juice and lemon derivatives against Vibrio cholerae." DOI: 10.1248/bpb.23.1235

9. Dias, D. (2007). "Homemade cleaners." Kansas State University. Retrieved from https://www.johnson.k-state.edu/docs/home-family/Homemade%20Cleaners.pdf

10. Najimu Nisha, S., et al. (2014). "Lemon peels mediated synthesis of silver

nanoparticles and its antidermatophytic activity." DOI: 10.1016/j.saa.2013.12.019

11. Qamaruz-Zaman, N. (2015). "Preliminary observation on the effect of baking soda volume on controlling odor from discarded organic waste." DOI: 10.1016/j.wasman.2014.09.017

12. Tyagi, R., et al. (2006). "Gels: Novel detergents for laundry applications." Retrieved from https://pdfs.semanticscholar.org/24bc/4bd63598a8d7c4c6d3c775a61eb705c88db1.pdf

13. Yagnik, D., et al. (2018). "Antimicrobial activity of apple cider vinegar against Escherichia coli, Staphylococcus aureus and Candida albicans; downregulating cytokine and microbial protein expression." DOI: 10.1038/s41598-017-18618-x

14. Yang, T. (2017). "Effectiveness of

commercial and homemade washing agents in removing pesticide residues on and in apples." Retrieved from https://pubs.acs.org/doi/pdf/10.1021/acs.jafc.7b03118

15. Zupancic, J., et al. (2016). "The black yeast Exophiala dermatitidis and other selected opportunistic human fungal pathogens spread from dishwashers to kitchens." PubMed Central. Retrieved from https://www.ncbi.nlm.nih.gov/pmc/articles/PMC4750988/

About Author

Kira Kendall, the author of "Organizing Your Home" is a retired telecommunications professional who has dedicated her life to helping others. At the age of 70, Kira has accumulated a wealth of knowledge and experience, drawing from her personal journey of transforming her own cluttered spaces into serene sanctuaries.

Born and raised on a small farm in Tennessee, Kira developed a strong work ethic and an appreciation for simplicity from an early age. During pursuing her career in telecommunications, she spent 11 years living in the area outside the city of Chicago. While there, she experienced firsthand the challenges of adapting to the city's weather, a stark contrast to her rural upbringing in the south.

With a family-oriented mindset, Kira successfully raised three beautiful daughters and is now blessed with nine grandchildren spanning various ages, from adulthood to grammar school. Family has always been a cornerstone of her life, and her experiences amidst the joys and chaos of raising children provided her with invaluable insights.

Kira's love for travel has taken her to various destinations, but her heart is particularly drawn to the beach. Whenever she has the opportunity, she indulges in the calming presence of the ocean, finding solace and inspiration in its vastness. This passion for exploration has cultivated a sense of adventure within her, which she brings to her writing and teachings.

An avid seamstress since childhood, Kira's mother introduced her to the art of sewing at the tender age of five. While she no longer makes clothes, she has found a deep passion for quilting and quilts. The artistry and attention to detail required in quilting resonates with her desire for precision and order, qualities she seeks to instill in her readers.

Kira's personal struggle with clutter and disorganization has been the driving force behind her mission to help others reclaim control over their living spaces. Through her own journey of learning to let go of unnecessary possessions, she discovered the freedom and peace of mind that comes with a simplified lifestyle. This transformation inspired her to share her experiences, insights, and practical strategies with others, leading her to write "Organizing Your Home."

Currently, Kira resides in a small town outside of Atlanta, Georgia, alongside her husband and her older sister. Together, they enjoy the tranquility of their wooded surroundings and continue in their pursuit of a harmonious lifestyle.

Kira Kendal's book, "Organizing Your Home," is a testament to her passion for helping others create a peaceful living environment. Through her expertise and compassionate approach, she aims to empower readers to embark on their own journeys of decluttering and finding the freedom that comes with an organized home.

Printed in Great Britain
by Amazon